David Fraser Harris

Saint Cecilia's Hall in the Niddry Wynd

A chapter in the history of the music of the past in Edinburgh

David Fraser Harris

Saint Cecilia's Hall in the Niddry Wynd
A chapter in the history of the music of the past in Edinburgh

ISBN/EAN: 9783337204372

Printed in Europe, USA, Canada, Australia, Japan

Cover: Foto ©ninafisch / pixelio.de

More available books at **www.hansebooks.com**

Saint Cecilia's Hall

IN THE NIDDRY WYND

A CHAPTER IN THE HISTORY
OF THE MUSIC OF THE PAST
IN EDINBURGH

BY DAVID FRASER HARRIS

M.D., C.M., B.SC. (LOND.), F.R.S.E., F.S.A. SCOT.
LECTURER ON PHYSIOLOGY IN THE
UNIVERSITY OF ST. ANDREWS

PUBLISHED BY
OLIPHANT ANDERSON AND FERRIER
EDINBURGH AND LONDON
1899

DEDICATED

TO

A. P. M.

A TRUE POET

AND

AS TRUE A FRIEND

PREFACE

It is commonly said that no one nowadays reads a preface. If this be true, I am indeed sorry, as it is here that I desire to tender my sincere thanks to Mr. Andrew Cairns, the present owner of St. Cecilia's Hall, for allowing me on several occasions to inspect the old place; to Mr. Ramsay, of Messrs. John C. Brodie and Sons, W.S., for his kindness in permitting me to examine title-deeds; to the officials in the Advocates' Library, Edinburgh, and in the Library of the University of Glasgow, for their patient courtesy in supplying me with the many books which I had from time to time to consult.

It also gives me much pleasure to express my indebtedness to Mr. Robert A. Marr, C.A., Edinburgh, than whom probably no one in Scotland knows more of the rise of choral societies. Mr. Marr not only furnished me with copies of his works on musical subjects, but placed at my disposal, for purposes of illustration in this work, his interesting collection of portraits of musicians, as well as several unique musical relics, amongst which I would specially mention the *manuscript* copy of the 'Index to the whole Musick belonging to the Edinburgh Musical Society, 1782.' From this precious volume, the only one of its kind, and therefore absolutely unreplaceable, Mr. Marr gave permission to reproduce the page we thought the most interesting.

To Mr. John Glen, musical-instrument maker, Edinburgh, my sincere thanks are due for his kindness in critically reading Chapter IV., which deals with subjects—foreign musicians in Edinburgh and the origin of Scottish song-tunes—upon which, from his life-long study of them, he can speak with indisputable authority.

CONTENTS

	PAGE
PREFACE	vii
LIST OF ILLUSTRATIONS	xi
BIBLIOGRAPHY	xiii

CHAPTER I
THE LOCALITY 1

CHAPTER II
THE BUILDING, AND THE NAME . . . 13

CHAPTER III
THE ARCHITECT 42

CHAPTER IV
THE PLAYERS AND THE SINGERS IN ST. CECILIA'S HALL   51

CHAPTER V
THE MUSIC PERFORMED AND SUNG IN ST. CECILIA'S HALL 160

CHAPTER VI

VARIOUS ACCOUNTS OF THE OLD EDINBURGH CONCERTS 191

CHAPTER VII

THE AUDIENCE 224

CHAPTER VIII

THE RISE AND DEVELOPMENT OF THE CONCERT IN
    EDINBURGH 248

APPENDICES 285

INDEX 301

LIST OF ILLUSTRATIONS

	PAGE
SMALL PLAN OF EDINBURGH SHOWING POSITION OF NIDDRY STREET	5
ST. MARY'S CHAPEL IN NIDDRY WYND	10
EXTERIOR OF ST. CECILIA'S HALL AT THE PRESENT TIME	15
OLD PLAN OF NIDDRY'S WYND	18
PART OF EDGAR'S PLAN OF THE CITY OF EDINBURGH	23
GROUND-FLOOR PLAN OF HALL	28
FIRST-FLOOR PLAN OF HALL	31
ST. CECILIA'S HALL AS DR. BELL'S SCHOOL	37
ROBERT MYLNE, THE ARCHITECT	43
GEORGE THOMSON	53
SIGNOR PUPPO	61
J. G. C. SCHETKY	71
SIGNOR STABILINI	85
WILHELM CRAMER	93
J. B. CRAMER	97
STEPHEN CLARKE	103

	PAGE
SIGNOR TENDUCCI	109
MDLLE. BACCHELLI	133
MUSICIANS' GROUP FROM STEWART WATSON'S PICTURE— NO. 2, SIGNOR CORRI	139
CORRI'S CONCERT-ROOMS	145
THOMAS ALEXANDER ERSKINE, SIXTH EARL OF KELLY	155
FACSIMILE PAGE FROM THE INDEX OF THE MUSIC BELONGING TO THE EDINBURGH MUSICAL SOCIETY, 1782	163
CORELLI	167
METASTASIO	171
DR. ARNE	175
I. J. PLEYEL	183
FACSIMILE OF TITLE-PAGE OF PROGRAMME OF LORD DRUMMORE'S FUNERAL CONCERT	207
TOMB OF JOHN FREDERICK LAMPE, CANONGATE CHURCHYARD, EDINBURGH	269

BIBLIOGRAPHY

History of Edinburgh. Hugo Arnot.
History of Edinburgh. Maitland.
History of Edinburgh. Kincaid.
Memorials of Edinburgh in the Olden Time. Wilson. A. and C. Black, Edinburgh and London, 1891.
Old and New Edinburgh. Grant. Cassell.
Edinburgh Life a Hundred Years Ago. Brown, Edinburgh, 1886.
Old Edinburgh Beaux and Belles. Paterson, Edinburgh, 1886.
Traditions of Edinburgh. Chambers, Edinburgh, 1868.
Letters from Edinburgh. Topham.
New Lights on Old Edinburgh. Reid.
Domestic Annals of Scotland. R. Chambers.
Annals of the Edinburgh Stage. J. C. Dibdin.
Memorials of My Time. Cockburn.
Journal (continuation of *Memorials*). Cockburn.
Life and Works of Daniel Defoe.
Letters of Robert Burns. Logie Robertson. W. Scott, London, 1887.

Poems of Robert Burns. Paterson, Edinburgh.
Life of Robert Burns. J. S. Blackie. W. Scott, London
Poems of Allan Ramsay. Gardner, Paisley, 1877.
Life of Allan Ramsay. Logie Robertson. W. Scott, London, 1887.
Life and Works of Smollett.
Life of Robert Fergusson. Grossart. (Famous Scots Series.) Oliphant, Anderson, and Ferrier, London and Edinburgh, 1898.
Life of Andrew Fletcher of Saltoun. G. W. T. Omond. (Famous Scots Series.)
Life of George Thomson. J. C. Hadden, London, 1898.
The Master-Masons of Scotland. Mylne.
Recollections of a Tour. O'Keefe.
History of Music. Dr. Charles Burney.
Musical Scotland. Baptie. Parlane, Paisley, 1894.
Lyric Poetry and Music of Scotland. Stenhouse. Blackwood, 1873.
Musical Memoirs. Parkes. London, 1830.
Life of Scott. J. G. Lockhart.
Dictionary of Musicians. 2 vols. Printed for Sainsbury and Co., Salisbury Square, Fleet Street, London, 1824.
Dictionary of Music and Musicians. 4 vols. Grove, 1879.
Biographical Dictionary of Musicians. Brown. Gardner.
Music for the People. R. A. Marr. Menzies and Co., Edinburgh, 1889.

Bibliography xv

Music and Musicians at the Edinburgh International Exhibition, 1886. R. A. Marr.

Programmes of the Concerts, Edinburgh Exhibition, 1890. R. A. Marr.

History of Music. Naumann, edited by the Rev. Sir F. A. Gore Ouseley, Bart.

History of the Lodge Canongate Kilwinning No. 2. Allan M'Kenzie.

Musical Memoirs of Scotland. Sir J. G. Dalzell.

Life of John C. Schetky, late Marine Painter in Ordinary to Her Majesty, by his daughter.

A Winter with Burns, 1786-87.

Edinburgh Evening Courant, 1720 to 1800.

Shepherd's Modern Athens displayed in a Series of Views. Jones and Co., London, 1831.

Caledonian Mercury.

Scots Magazine.

History of Freemasonry and the Grand Lodge of Scotland. Wm. A. Laurie.

Freemasonry in Scotland. D. Murray Lyon.

Picture of Edinburgh. J. Stark, 1806.

CHAPTER I

THE LOCALITY

THE stranger in Edinburgh, perchance on some dull grey day when the bitter East pours its misty breath over the already dark wynds and closes of the ancient Scottish capital, may be pardoned, as he trudges down the old High Street, for casting merely a passing glance at the modern, japanned tinplate bearing the apparently totally uninteresting words, 'Niddry Street.' He would not by any means be so readily pardoned if he still showed indifference when we told him that in a hall still existing at the foot of that street there used to regularly assemble, in the days of long ago, a brilliant company of high-born dames and the leading men of the period, to listen to concerts of classical and national music rendered by an orchestra, professional and amateur, the most eminent that the time could produce. The very walls still stand that vibrated to the strains of the *Messiah* as a *new* oratorio, that echoed to the tenor of Tenducci and the falsetto of Corri; in this very hall an old gentleman was overheard to say, on hearing for the first time a sonata of Haydn's, 'Poor new-fangled stuff!—I hope we shall never hear it again'; that very cupola looked down upon the flirtations of the beautiful Eglantine Maxwell, saw behind the facile fan of Jane, Duchess of Gordon, and watched the rhythm of the melody flush the damask cheek of the heavenly Miss Burnet with a matchlessly delicate hue.

It seems a 'far cry' from the once narrow, tortuous, sunless alley of the Niddry Wynd, with its tall, age-stained 'lands' shutting out the daylight of the cold northern sky, to the bright, sun-bathed Italian city of Parma, lit by the smiles of an eternal blue; and yet there is one link of direct association, for the architect of St. Cecilia's Hall built it on the model of the opera-house of Parma. The Teatro Farnese of Parma, long very ruinous, was a wooden structure erected in the years 1618 and 1619 from the designs of Aleotti d'Argenta. It held 4500 persons. The Edinburgh of the sixteenth, seventeenth, and eighteenth centuries was by no means that isolated, out-of-the-world place which some suppose it: its younger sons had for generations supplied soldiers for a Royal Guard at the court of France; its best-loved, girl-widow queen had come straight from Paris to the Port of Leith; that queen's father had been married in Notre-Dame; that queen's son brought his bride by sea from Denmark; the battlefields of Sweden and Holland knew the Scottish veterans almost better than did their patrimonial castles; the Guises were as familiar with Edinburgh as with their duchy; the greatest Scottish reformer knew Geneva and Frankfort as well as he knew St. Andrews and the Netherbow; and the most familiar cry in the streets of Edinburgh was a corruption of a French phrase.

The Old Edinburgh of to-day, with sombre grey sandstone and absence of bright colour alike on its houses and its inhabitants, presents a very different appearance artistically from that of mediæval Edinburgh, which, if indeed its sky was so often as leaden as ours—a thing to be seriously doubted,—was a city of brilliant colouring on roofs, balconies, timber-fronts, pillars, piazzas, and outside stairs; while its frequent royal, ecclesiastic, and civic processions would ever and anon fill its crowded streets with new elements of chromatism.

To all this, add the gaily coloured dress of peers and peasants, burghers and country visitors, and you have a scene full of all possible colour-combinations, some of which no doubt would have scandalised the modern æsthete; for as the sounds of drawn swords would have clashed in his ears, so would colours in his eyes, on the venerable High Street. A modern might doubtless find that colours 'killed' each other in those days as readily as men did.

Niddry Street is the first on the right-hand side as you descend the High Street from where 'The Bridges' cross it at the Tron Church, and has been known as a *street* since about 1788, when the wynd of mediæval times was entirely swept away during the formation of that great piece of engineering, the South Bridge.

A large number of very old, and no doubt very insanitary, but at the same time historical and picturesque, mansions were pulled down to make way for monotonous and commonplace blocks of houses. The wynd had been, in a Pickwickian sense, 'improved,' but improved off the face of the earth. Into the vexed question of how far, in a city like Edinburgh, we are warranted in listening to the claims of Hygiene while remaining deaf to those of History, Æstheticism, and Archæology, we must not at present enter: suffice it to say that, for the last thirty years, 'Ichabod' may be said to have been 'writ large' upon the sky of the Niddry Wynd. Although we may discover many a more romantic and historical locality in Old Edinburgh, Niddry Wynd has had its full share of both romance and history.

First as to the name itself: there can be little doubt that the ground on which the wynd came to be built was the intramural possession of some landed proprietor of the name of Niddry. In charters of David II. a Henry Niddry is mentioned, and in

The Locality

those of Robert III. a John Niddry is found owning land both at Cramond and at Pentland Muir. The

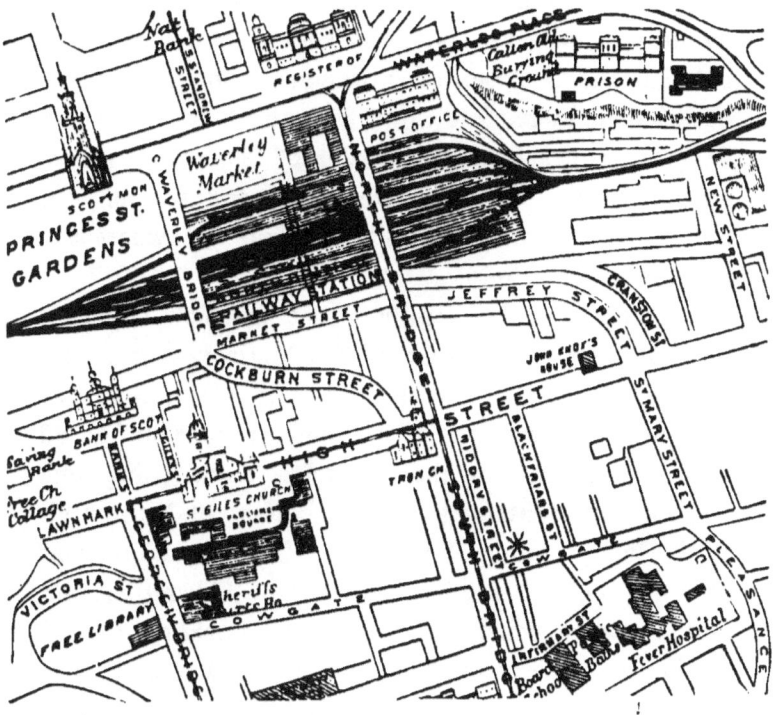

SMALL PLAN OF EDINBURGH SHOWING POSITION OF NIDDRY STREET.
* SAINT CECILIA'S HALL.

Wauchopes of Niddry[1] in Midlothian — the oldest family in the county, having come to Scotland in the

[1] The family of the gallant soldier, General Wauchope, of the Khartoum Campaign (1898).

eleventh century with Margaret, queen of Malcolm Canmore—have evidently existed long enough to have had a town-house in this wynd so named from the circumstance—a very common source of the names of old Edinburgh closes, *e.g.* Strichen's from the Frasers of Strichen, Tweeddale Court from the Hays of Tweeddale, Liberton's from the Littles of Liberton, Warriston's from the lairds of Warriston, and so on. In the reign of James III., Niddry Wynd was where the Salt Market was held.

The most notable family whose mansion stood in the wynd itself was that of Lockhart of Carnwath, the head of which at the time of the Union was George Lockhart (born 1673, died 1731), who figured very prominently in those stirring days, being one of four representatives for the county of Edinburgh in the last Scottish Parliament. Their mansion was built in 1591 by a Nicol Edward or Udward, round four sides of a court (later known as Lockhart Court) on the west side of the wynd about half-way down. It was demolished in 1785 to allow of the construction of the South Bridge, the new southern approach to the city. According to the late Sir Daniel Wilson, this house seems to have been one of the most magnificent residences of the old town, which is saying a good deal, for at this date almost every wynd had in it one or more houses very richly decorated. The Lockharts of Carnwath must be distinguished from the Lockharts of Lee, whose mansion was in Old Bank Close. In what was later the Lockhart mansion, James VI. and Anne of Denmark were entertained, at their own request, in January 1591 by Nicol Edward. King James was often the self-invited guest of his wealthy subjects, and had been indeed entertained in another house in this same wynd in 1584 by Provost Black of Balbi. This latter place was nearer the 'heid o' the wynd,' and it was from here that the King walked in state to hold a Parliament in the Old Tolbooth. From the Lockhart mansion it was that the Earl of Huntly, on February 7, 1593, fled to a deed of blood—the murder of the 'Bonny Earl of Moray' at Donibristle, while at a much later date there lived here Bruce of Kinnaird, the famous traveller to the sources of the Nile (1770).

The old Niddry Wynd was likewise the home in the metropolis of another Scottish family, the mention of whose name recalls a tale of violence and mystery—the Erskines of Grange. Their mansion stood on the other side, almost opposite Lockhart Court. The story is a well-known one in Edinburgh annals under the title 'Banishment of Lady Grange'; but the lady in question had in reality no title, being the wife of the Hon. James Erskine, a Lord of Session with the judicial or territorial title of Lord Grange. James V., who instituted the College of Justice, while admitting that he had 'made the carls Lords,' once asked, 'Wha the deil made the carlines Ladies?' We have thus the matter of titles of the wives of Lords of Session settled by one who was perhaps the chief lady's-man in a dynasty which cannot be truthfully reproached with lack of gallantry.

Told as briefly as possible, the story is that Lord Grange, after thirty years of wedded life, banished his wife to the remote island of St. Kilda, where he kept her a prisoner for seven years. It seems pretty clearly proved that the lady was carried off with considerable violence from her house in the Niddry Wynd by certain persons in the service of Simon Fraser, Lord Lovat, a man whose own record in matters matrimonial was highly discreditable.

Lord Grange talked of the affair as a 'sequestration,' under which guise it almost appears as though he had done something heroic; but the fact that a Lord of Session so lately as 1732 could with impunity banish his wife, without even the semblance of a trial, to a lonely island, is not only a curious commentary upon the temper and manners of legal luminaries of that period, but is a striking indication of the hypnotic state of public opinion.

The ecclesiastical antiquities of the wynd are not without interest. At the time Arnot wrote his *History*

(1779) there still stood, a little below Lockhart Court and on the opposite side, an ancient chapel—St. Mary's—dedicated to God and the Blessed Virgin, and built in 1505 by 'Elizabeth, Countess of Ross.'[1] In 1618 the Corporation of Wrights and Masons purchased it, and for long used it as their place of meeting. Later they came to be known as the 'United Incorporations of Mary's Chapel,' and in Arnot's time were meeting in the old place. Not long afterwards a new chapel was built, and was the scene of certain religious services in 1770 promoted by the zealous Lady Glenorchy. In 1779 the Rev. John Logan of South Leith, a poet of some repute in his day, gave a course of lectures in the chapel upon the 'Philosophy of History,' prior to offering himself as a candidate for the Chair of Civil History in the University of Edinburgh.

Even in the days of the original chapel, the Freemasons had met in it, and there has for long existed 'a masonic lodge of Mary's Chapel.' There met the Musical Society, which was not only the direct predecessor but the parent of the St. Cecilia's Society, for whom the hall was built at the foot of the wynd. We shall have a good deal to say of this

---

[1] Grant's *Old and New Edinburgh*. She was by her first marriage fifth Countess of Errol, and Baroness Ross by a second marriage.

Society when tracing the development of the Concert in Edinburgh.

ST. MARY'S CHAPEL IN NIDDRY WYND.
(*From an Engraving in Maitland's 'History of Edinburgh.'*)

The Niddry Wynd is always mentioned in connection with Allan Ramsay's first Edinburgh house and shop 'at the sign of the Mercury opposite the head of the Niddry Wynd.' Prior to 1725 he here conducted his business; and it was here that he published the *Gentle Shepherd*—a work of which it has been well said, 'It has only *just* escaped being a classic.'

Again the Niddry Wynd figures in the short, sad life of Edinburgh's youthful poet, Robert Fergusson, better known, unfortunately, as Burns's model for metre than for anything he himself wrote. This Fergusson was born (5th September 1750) in the 'Cap and Feather Close' in a high 'land'[1] on the east side of Halkerston's Wynd, and was sent in 1756 naturally to the nearest school. This happened to be one somewhere in the Niddry Wynd, opened in 1750 by a Mr. Philp—'Teacher of English.'

The Niddry Wynd comes up in connection with the town-house of the noted Edinburgh surgeon, Benjamin Bell—one of the early luminaries who contributed to give the Edinburgh school of Medicine that prestige which to this day it has never lost. Writing in September 1777, he tells how he had 'got fixed at last in a very good house, well aired and lighted, with an easy access of one story from Niddry's Wynd, and an entry from Kinloch's Close without any stairs.' This Benjamin Bell was the great-grand-

---

[1] Demolished for the construction of the North Bridge.

father of the well-known and no less well-beloved Edinburgh surgeon of the present day, Dr. Joseph Bell, whose remarkable intuitions with regard to his patients suggested to his pupil Conan Doyle the character which he afterwards amplified as 'Sherlock Holmes.' St. Cecilia's Hall extended from the Niddry Wynd on the west through to Dickson's Close on the east, both the wynd and the close running between the High Street and the Cowgate. Kinloch's Close, which also descended from the High Street towards the Cowgate, did not extend further than the north elevation of St. Mary's Chapel, and was thus not a thoroughfare.[1]

[1] For the position of these closes see Edgar's plan, page 23.

CHAPTER II

THE BUILDING, AND THE NAME

THE St. Cecilia's Hall of to-day, numbered prosaically as '40 Niddry Street' in the Post-Office Directory, must present a good deal of difference externally from what it did when it formed a portion of the southern end of the eastern side of Niddry's Wynd. For the present Niddry Street is not exactly upon the site of Niddry's Wynd,[1] which was further to the west than is the line of the existing street.

As you descend from the High Street, you notice on the left-hand side a smoke-stained building jutting out into the street, and thereby causing the pavement on the east side to come to an abrupt ending. On looking up at this edifice you notice at once it is different in character from the neighbouring houses, and that—with its Grecian pediment surmounting the west wall—it has, as viewed from this, the front elevation, an indefinable air of having seen better days. Our illustration

---

[1] Contrary to what is stated in *Old and New Edinburgh*, Grant, p. 245, vol. ii.

suggests this appearance of faded grandeur, which an inspection of the place confirms, for that entrance, shown with its lintel and ornamental supports, which once admitted the exquisites of Edinburgh into a vestibule below their beautiful concert-room, leads you to-day into a stone-flagged storage-room filled with barrels and boxes.

The hall and the vestibule below it were built in 1762, on the site of a number of very old houses standing at the south-east corner of Niddry's Wynd, near its opening into the Cowgate.

Thus the position of the hall in relation to its surroundings is clearly stated in the following extract from 'An Act and Warrant,' dated 1760, of the Dean of Guild's Court of Edinburgh, in favour of the Musical Society for the erection of a hall:—' Anent the petition given by William Douglas, merchant in Edinburgh, treasurer to and in name of the Musical Society of Edinburgh, showing that the said Society had lately purchased and acquired several houses, and an area having an entry from the Cowgate by the close called Davidson's Close, and a separate entry by a large area entering from Niddry's Wynd, which whole area consists of 77 feet in length from North to South, and 46 feet in breadth ... the Musical Society intend to build a great hall, or musical house, upon the ground above mentioned ... attended with great expense,' etc. etc. etc.

SAINT CECILIA'S HALL AT THE PRESENT TIME.

The Building and the Name 17

Subject to the two following conditions, the Society was to be allowed to build the hall :—

1. The Musical Society was to provide a drain ('water-gang') to pass their hall, in order to carry away water from the higher grounds 'passed the chapel' (St. Mary's, belonging to the Incorporated Trades), for—'The Incorporations have a servitude upon the Society's said ground of a water-gang or free passage for water coming down from the higher grounds on the north side of the chapel.'

2. The Musical Society was not to make any passage or doorway, and not to open up an old one, long closed, between Davidson's property on the south and St. Mary's Chapel on the north of their ground.[1]

All these things being duly promised, the Dean of Guild, John Carmichael, and his council gave permission. For further details as to the formalities incident to this transaction see Appendix No. I.

The illustration on page 19, which is a reproduction of a portion of a plan in the possession of the City of Edinburgh, shows in darker lines the outline of St. Cecilia's Hall, from which it is clear that there were buildings on the western aspect of the hall both to the north and to the south of the entrance.

When these buildings came to be removed, to make way for the foundations of the houses which were to

[1] *F* in Edgar's plan, p. 23, is St. Mary's Chapel.

form the eastern side of South Bridge Street, the backs of which were to form the western side of Niddry Street, the whole of the western elevation of St. Cecilia's Hall was, for the first time, exposed to view. But, naturally, where these buildings had abutted on the hall, the wall of the latter would not have been so carefully finished as the central portion, which had a clear space in front of it, and contained the entrance; and the previously hidden portions, not having been faced in sandstone or ashlar-work like the part in the middle, were faced in plaster, to obliterate the raw or rough-finished appearance occasioned by the removal of these buildings. Hence it is that the northern and southern portions of the elevation towards Niddry Street have not a facing of ashlar-work.

The plan in the possession of the City of Edinburgh, of which we reproduce only a small part, is undated, or more probably the section bearing the date has been destroyed, as it does not seem to be complete. The measurement of each line on the plan is most accurately given[1] in feet and inches, and it has evidently been a careful survey for some important purpose, possibly for determining the best site for the South Bridge. In any case, whether prepared specially or not, it has been used for this purpose, as there

---

[1] For the sake of clearness we have omitted the measurements in our tracing.

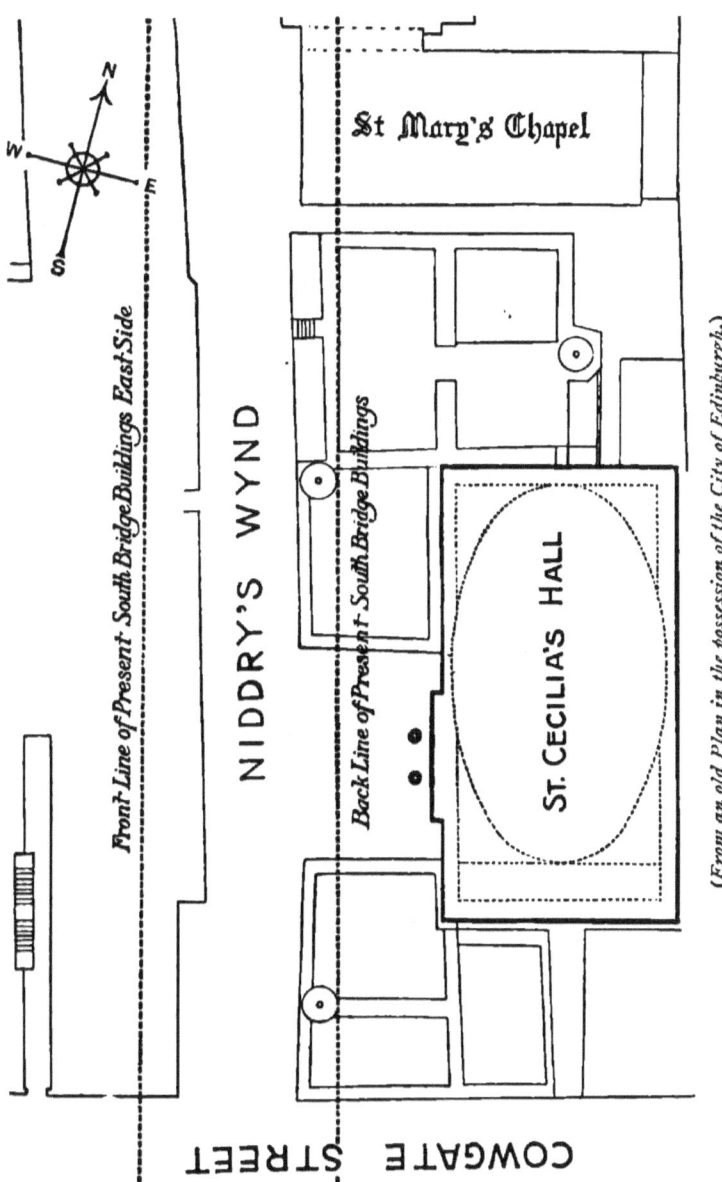

(From an old Plan in the possession of the City of Edinburgh.)

are a number of pencil-lines drawn across it corresponding with the present position of South Bridge Street and Hunter Square. Two of these pencil-lines, which, by careful inspection of the Ordnance Survey Map of the present time, we have proved to correspond exactly with the *front* and *back* of the buildings on the east side of the South Bridge, are indicated on our reproduction by heavy dotted lines.

This clearly shows that the houses forming the eastern side of South Bridge Street stand upon the ground occupied by the line of Niddry's Wynd, and that the present Niddry Street passes right through the site of houses which formed the eastern side of the wynd. Thus both sides of Niddry's Wynd were demolished—not the eastern side only, as Grant's *Old and New Edinburgh* would lead us to believe.[1]

The position of the famous St. Mary's Chapel is shown in the plan, and it will be seen that the line of the South Bridge Street buildings is carried right through the chapel.

The operations in connection with that truly great triumph of engineering skill—the South Bridge—lasted from 1785 to 1788, when South Bridge Street was opened for vehicular traffic.

Hence among the papers and title-deeds pertaining to the property of the Musical Society we read of the

[1] Vol. ii. p. 374.

'loss and damage sustained by the formation of Niddry Street and the South Bridge,' in consequence of which it is recorded that the 'Trustees of the South Bridge in 1787 gave as a recompense to the Directors (of the Musical Society) a small area fronting the Cowgate, on the south-east side of St. Cecilia's Hall, as well as the area between the hall and the Cowgate.'

Another document speaks of the directors of the Musical Society 'having agreed to the widening of Niddry Street, by which the entry to the hall was much hurt,' which we can quite well understand must have been so, when we remember that, as the plan shows, the whole western side of the wynd was to be pulled down, and much of the eastern side, after which the houses flanking the great bridge of nineteen arches were to be erected.

The inconvenience occasioned by the extensive operations in the wynd was such that for a time the regular concerts of the Musical Society, or, as it now occasionally called itself, the 'Harmonical Society,' had to be held in another building. In the *Edinburgh Evening Courant* of June 7th, 1787, there occurs the following :—'Harmonical Society. The access to St. Cecilia's Hall, in which the meetings of the Harmonical Society have hitherto been held, being rendered extremely incommodious by the taking down the tenements at the foot of Niddry's Wynd, the next

FROM THE PLAN OF THE CITY AND CASTLE OF EDINBURGH, BY WILLIAM EDGAR, ARCHITECT, 1765.

19 St. Cecilia's Hall.
78 Nidrie's Wynd.
79 Kinloch's Close.
80 Dickson's Close.
81 Cant's Close.
B Tolbooth.
F St. Mary's Chapel.
L The Market Cross.
M The Town Guard House.

The Building and the Name   25

meeting will be held, Monday next the 11th of June current, in St. John's Lodge, Canongate, at seven in the evening, and the meetings will be thereafter regularly continued once a fortnight till further notice.'

Two other wynds disappeared at this time—Marlin's and Peebles' Wynds—Hunter Square and Blair Street partly replacing them.

From our reproduction of the well-known map of Edinburgh by Edgar, published in 1765, the position of St. Cecilia's Hall in the Niddry Wynd can be clearly made out.

The original map by William Edgar, architect, was published in 1742, and gives Niddry's Wynd with, of course, no St. Cecilia's Hall; but in the new edition of 1765, which was issued with a note—'*N.B.* All the new buildings, etc., are expressed in this plan to the present year by an eminent architect'—one can very easily see where the copperplate has been altered to indicate the position of the concert-hall erected three years before. It is possible to make out this in our reproduction of a portion of the map.[1]

Another interesting feature of this second edition of the map is that it shows the proposed new North Bridge, one of the piers of which had been founded at this time (1765). It is explained in the index that

---

[1] The original copperplate of Edgar's map is in the possession of Mr. David Johnstone, 47A Hanover Street, Edinburgh.

'the dott'd lines show ye Road along ye intended Bridge.'

The closes or wynds in this locality, as at 1765, were, passing from west to east, Peebles', Marlin's, Niddry's, Kinloch's, Dickson's, and Cant's.

The building of St. Cecilia's itself comprises two distinct portions, one on the level of the street—the ground-floor—and the concert-hall proper on the floor above. We give an illustration of each, and in the plan of the ground-floor the space marked 'entrance' is the ornamental doorway in Niddry Street in front of which, apparently, judging from the plan in the possession of the City of Edinburgh, there formerly existed two pillars, no trace of which is now visible.

This ground-floor space is found to be divided into three portions by two transverse structures, the northern of which consists of three arches, while the southern is at present a wall, but in all probability was originally arched like its neighbour.

On very close examination we could make out appearances indicating arches filled in with masonry, and then plastered over so that there is a bulging along the curved line of the inside of each arch.

Towards the south end of this ground-floor space or vestibule, as we might call it—for it is difficult to find a single term that is applicable,—we see in the plan the indications of four pillars. The shafts of these are of

The Building and the Name 27

stone—monoliths indeed—and are by no means slender, for they support the 'landing' of the upper floor, to which access is gained by the two staircases indicated east and west of the pillars.

The capitals of the pillars are of wood boldly carved to represent hanging bunches of fruit of some sort amidst leaves, the whole being so heavily whitewashed over that these details were not made out until we had scraped off more than one coating of the plaster or limy material.

Of the two staircases only the western one is intact, its neighbour having evidently been long ago built up during the course of one of the many transformations which this old place has undergone since 1800.

The east wall of this vestibule is also not solid but arched, as many as four arches being yet observable.

These arched spaces, for they are not cellars, make excellent dry storage-room, and for this purpose the owner of the hall has let them.

There can be little doubt this arched and pillared vestibule served the purpose of a lobby, under-hall, or place of assembling for those attending a concert.

Into this place, protected from wind and rain, and after dark lit up by lamps, the sedan-chairs would be carried, so that the ladies could alight in comfort without the risk of having their finery soiled; no rushing across a rain-splashed pavement, ruining satin shoes, and, with skirts gathered up, more like the proverbial

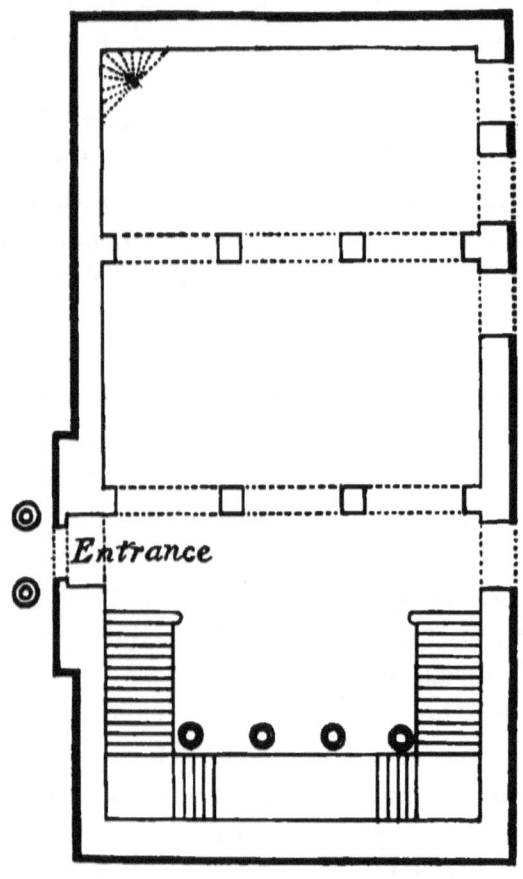

GROUND-FLOOR PLAN OF ST. CECILIA'S HALL.

'hen on the hot girdle' than anything human. Down here, too, people could greet and meet one another;

The Building and the Name 29

there were friends to be recognised and parties made up before going into the hall upstairs. Similarly, on leaving the place, the chairs could be brought into the vestibule and the fair burdens carried off, attended by the link-men or 'flambeaux-bearers,' in a state of at least physical comfort—the mental comfort would depend upon how many women had just been seen considered to be better dressed than the 'fair burden' in question.

The staircase, which is still open, is wonderfully easy of ascent, the steps being low and broad: at the place indicated on the plan there is a stone landing whence the steps are continued up, at right angles to the first portion, on to the landing of the concert-hall.

Here, then, are the original steps leading to this most famous of concert-rooms—worn indeed, in places almost worn away altogether, and now piled high with boxes, baskets, packing-cases, hampers, packages and bundles, but still there—still there, the very steps that during the last four decades of last century must have been trodden by almost every well-known person in Scottish society.

Lords and ladies, judges and advocates, musical connoisseurs, artistic critics, men of letters, men of science, men of business, men of leisure, distinguished foreign visitors—any that were anybody and some that were certainly somebody—perhaps Arne, Smollett,

Burns, Hume, Dr. Johnson, Boswell, Mackenzie, Walter Scott, and the Duc de Berri—passed up and down these same old stone stairs on which we are now standing! Did the 'Flower of Strathmore' actually tread these steps?—certainly, unless it was the set built up on the other side!

We may now pass to our plan of the hall itself: this shows the famous 'oval' mentioned in nearly all the descriptions of the place.

The stairs converged on a landing, only five feet ten inches wide, which led by two stone steps to the door of the hall.

At the north end of the oval, opposite the entrance, stood the organ behind the space for the orchestra: the seats, we are told, were ranged amphitheatrically round the hall, leaving a space in the centre where the people could walk about during the intervals.

No doubt the rows of seats in tiers followed the curve of the great ellipse, except at the end near the door, where there may have been an opening admitting the audience to the central space. Thomson, however, describes 'a passage a few feet broad that was carried quite round the hall behind the last of the elevated seats,' from which we may infer that on arriving in the hall you could go round through this passage to the orchestra or north end, and then, turning back, proceed to your seat, as is still the way in many halls and theatres where the stall seats are entered

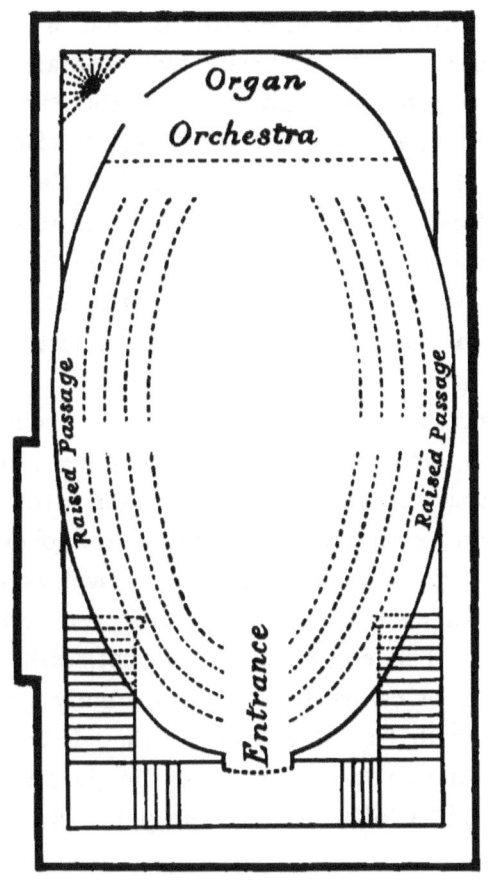

FIRST-FLOOR PLAN OF ST. CECILIA'S HALL.

from the front or stage end only. Perhaps, as we

have suggested in the plan, there were short straight passages between the seats at intervals.

In Thomson's account we are told that the musicians gained access to the orchestra by a separate staircase not visible from the auditorium: of this structure no trace is left, unless we regard an obliquely placed beam in the roof of the north-west corner of the vestibule below the hall as having been erected in this position to support the joists and give a free space for the staircase. It was probably a wooden structure, and has long ago disappeared, but we have indicated on the plan its supposed position.

A visitor to-day to the interior of St. Cecilia's Hall will see no trace whatever of its having been oval; the internal space is rectangular,[1] the walls meet at right angles, and yet the reproduction of the plan of the locality on p. 19 distinctly shows the oval, *carried into the east and west walls*, within an outer rectangular structure. The elliptical arched roof, with its truly oval cupola or centre light, has apparently never been interfered with from the inside, although the present ventilator of zinc on the outside of the glass was almost certainly added after the concert period was over, *i.e.* after 1800.

The small gallery at the south end represented in the

[1] Present dimensions: length, 63 feet 3 inches; breadth, 35 feet 6 inches; height to moulding on cornice, 17 feet 10 inches.

The Building and the Name 33

view of the hall on page 37, was probably not present in the days of the concerts, but subsequently added, possibly by the Freemasons, to whose alterations on the place we shall shortly allude.

It certainly never was the 'musicians' gallery,' as some writers on the hall have conjectured, because orchestra, harpsichord, and organ were all together at the *north* end, and because there could have been no room for an organ in a gallery so near the ceiling.

Quite different is the state of matters in the large Freemasons' Hall in George Street, where there is certainly a 'musicians' gallery,' large enough to accommodate not only musicians but the organ too.

With the history of what went on between 1762 and 1800 in the hall thus described we have no concern in this chapter dealing exclusively with the fabric and the changes wrought on it. Amongst the papers relative to the property, there is one dated June 5, 1801, entitled—'Articles of Roup and Sale by Musical Society of St. Cecilia's Hall, and two areas in the Cowgate, and enactment thereon, in favour of Mr. James Gibson, W.S.,' which shows that the end of something had come.

Appended to this paper are one or two rather interesting signatures, viz., those of David Rae, Lord Eskgrove, whom Cockburn and Sir Walter Scott used to make such fun of, as also of Sir William Forbes of

Pitsligo, and Gilbert Innes of Stow, who, as we know, was one of the directors of the Musical Society.

In 1802, St. Cecilia's Hall became the property of the members of the Baptist Communion, and doubtless they altered it internally in some way to suit the rather different purpose to which they were to put it. No trace of anything resembling a pulpit or platform remains to-day.

In 1809 it changed hands, for we find it recorded:[1] 'At a meeting on 18th August 1809, it was reported that St. Cecilia's Hall, Niddry Street, had been purchased by the Substitute Grand Master, William Inglis, Alexander Lawrie, and James Bartram, Esqrs., on the part of the Grand Lodge of Scotland, for the purpose of converting it into a Freemasons' Hall, at the price of £1400, which purchase was unanimously approved of.'

From the very first, then, the Freemasons contemplated making alterations upon the hall, but it seems these were not immediately commenced, for the hall was 'consecrated' upon 21st November 1809, as we read:[2] 'On 21st November 1809, the Free Masons' Hall of Scotland was consecrated.'

This ceremony over, a committee was appointed to take charge of the necessary alterations, and on 5th

---

[1] *History of Freemasonry and the Grand Lodge of Scotland*, by William A. Lawrie, p. 177.   [2] *Ibid.* p. 180.

The Building and the Name 35

November 1810 it was reported by the committee in charge that the alterations were completed.

It may have been during these alterations that the walls giving the oval form to the interior were removed, and that the gallery was constructed. Possibly the large cupboard in the east wall was constructed to utilise the space in the outer wall when the oval wall was taken down.

In June 1811 the Baptists removed to their 'new meeting-house in the Pleasance,' and from Masonic records it would seem that, although they sold the place to the Freemasons in 1809, they still used the hall for their services for two years more.

No sooner had the Baptists left, and the Freemasons begun to meet in their hall so lately altered to suit them, than they seem to have found it too small for due exercise in their stimulating mysteries. We find, on 5th March 1812, a petition lodged in the Dean of Guild Court, Edinburgh, on behalf of the Grand Lodge of Freemasons, for making an addition to the building at the foot of Niddry Street, formerly called St. Cecilia's Hall, now 'Free Masons' Hall.'

They desired to build on 'the piece of vacant ground lying on the south of said hall, the length of Cowgate Street.'[1] What they did build was an additional hall on the level of St. Cecilia's Hall, with an inside

[1] See Appendix No. II.

entrance to it from the landing which formerly gave access only to St. Cecilia's: this additional hall rested on shops, or a shop—at present a public-house, 214 Cowgate.

At the level of the roof of the new or additional hall, on the side overlooking the Cowgate, we accordingly find 'Free Masons' Hall, 1812,' carved on a rectangular stone tablet.

This extra hall, and the shops below, were merely built on to the southern end of St. Cecilia's, *i.e.* only three new walls and a roof had to be provided.

This renovated and enlarged St. Cecilia's Hall formed the home for thirty-five years (*i.e.* from 1809 to 1844) of the Grand Lodge of Freemasons of Scotland. Thus in *Freemasonry in Scotland*[1] we read of 'St. Cecilia's Hall, where the Grand Lodge of Scotland was for thirty-five years accustomed to hold its meetings, having in 1809 purchased the building for £1400, and converted it into a Freemasons' Hall.'

But once again '*tempora mutantur*'; exeunt Freemasons! In 1844 the Town Council of Edinburgh purchased the whole property of the Freemasons in Niddry Street, with the intention of locating a school for young children in it.

'For some time negotiations had been going on for the purchase of the Grand Lodge property in

[1] D. Murray Lyon, p. 239.

ST. CECILIA'S HALL AFTER 1844 AS DR. BELL'S SCHOOL.

The Building and the Name 39

Niddry Street, by the Town Council of Edinburgh, for the purpose of converting it into a school under the trust-settlements of the late Dr. Bell, the founder of the Madras system of Education, and a Missive of Sale was signed in the City Chambers on the 10th day of October 1844, whereby the whole heritable property belonging to the Grand Lodge of Scotland at the foot of Niddry Street, comprising two halls, shops, etc., was disposed of at the price of £1800 sterling.'[1]

The two halls mentioned here are of course old Cecilia's and the smaller hall of 1812; the shops may refer to whatever was below the latter hall, and entered from the Cowgate, or it may allude to the arched space or vestibule entered from Niddry Street. Certain it is that at the present moment there is an entrance[2] (numbered 42) to the northern portion of this space, which is walled off from the southern portion, entered by the old or original entrance (numbered 44), and in this way two different shops or stores down here *could* have existed.

The illustration which we give from Grant's *Old and New Edinburgh* clearly belongs to this period, when school classes were held in the hall, the figures represented being those of little boys and their master.

[1] Wm. A. Lawrie, *History of Freemasonry and the Grand Lodge of Scotland*, p. 256.
[2] It is possible this was originally a window.

A portion of the famous cyclopæan cupola is well seen, and the gallery is shown with staircases at the ends.

The children probably used the arched space below as a playground at the time the classes were held in the hall above.

For many years past a firm of bookbinders and paper-rulers has been installed in this long-deserted 'hall of song.' To-day the rattle of machinery and the hum of busy workers has replaced the harmonies of the overture and the melodic solemnity of the oratorio; but possibly, to the ears of those who estimate all things at their value in £ s. d., these metallic sounds in the St. Cecilia of to-day may be 'sweeter sounds than music makes.' And so the pageant of life has marched through this old room: Singer, Peer, Beauty, Baptist Preacher, Right Worshipful Master, Dominie—your voices all are still,—' *Sic transit gloria mundi.*'

As to the name itself: St. Cecilia was a Roman virgin who suffered martyrdom in the beginning of the third century. Being so exquisite a player that even angels came down to listen to her, it was decided she was to 'wed music,' and in consequence she vowed perpetual virginity.

We are told, however, that, against her will, she was betrothed to a Pagan, Valerian, but that, having converted him to Christianity, she preserved the integrity of her vow. It was the early Roman Catholic Italian painters who regarded her as the 'patron saint of Music,' and the honour has been ascribed to her ever since. She is usually represented seated at an organ in a Gothic church, and clad more in keeping with her future celestial character than with her then existing earthly one. No doubt both the organ and St. Cecilia's wings are alike anticipatory.

St. Cecilia's Day, or the 'Feast of St. Cecilia,' is November 22nd. The late Professor Sir F. A. Gore Ouseley, Bart., Oxon., is of opinion that this saint *was* 'historical,' and came of the Roman patrician family Cæcilia. She is reported to have converted her judge to Christianity, and then to have suffered martyrdom in the reign of Marcus Aurelius, A.D. 177. For centuries a tomb in the Roman catacombs has been pointed out as that of St. Cecilia, and over it is a seventh-century fresco representing her in a richly embroidered 'stola,' the distinctive dress of the patricians. So many pilgrims flocked to her tomb during the early centuries of the Christian era, that the entrance to the crypt was used as a vestibule-chapel.

In Dresden there is a painting by Carlo Dolci of St. Cecilia playing the organ; in the Louvre one of her by Domenichino in which she plays a six-stringed 'bass,' the music being held by a cherub; while Bologna has a St. Cecilia by Raphael; but there are many others in the various galleries of Europe.

CHAPTER III

THE ARCHITECT

ROBERT MYLNE, F.R.S., who was born in Edinburgh in 1733 and died in London in 1811, was the architect of St. Cecilia's Hall. At the time that he designed the hall he was only thirty-one years of age, yet he had by that time studied architecture in Rome, and had won, amid the acclamations of judges and spectators, the first prize in the first class of architecture at the Academy of St. Luke in the 'Eternal City.' In the *Scots Magazine* for January 1759 there appeared a long poem in praise of the clever young architect. The friend's appreciation of Mylne's work was stronger than his poetical powers, so that we spare the reader the entire poem, which is not exactly within the limits of the Italian sonnet; we shall quote, we hope, judiciously:—

'ROME, *Sept.* 23*rd*, 1758.

'To Mr. Robert Mylne, of Edinburgh, on his obtaining the first prize in the first class of Architecture, from the Academy of St. Luke, at Rome, the 15th inst.

'By his friend, G. W.

ROBERT MYLNE, ARCHITECT.

(Reproduced, by kind permission of the Rev. R. S. Mylne, from the 'Master Masons of Scotland.')

'Accept, dear Mylne, nor like a critic view
The verse, to merit and to friendship due ;
   (*Concluding lines.*)
To cure the nation's taste be first your care ;
Then Britain will for long-lost arts declare,
Will raise the structure by your hand designed,
Will rival Rome—leave Rome, perhaps, behind ;
Will do you justice, and enrol your name
First in the book of everlasting fame.'

Robert Mylne came of a good old Scottish stock—men who had literally 'made their mark' (in the form of the mason's sign) upon many an enduring building throughout the length and breadth of Scotland. This Robert Mylne was the first of his family to seek professional occupation outside of Scotland, but he did it to such purpose in London that his plans were the accepted ones for Blackfriars Bridge over the Thames, and it was he who died as the superintendent of St. Paul's Cathedral, beneath whose majestic dome he lies buried, close to the tomb of Wren. It was Mylne who composed the famous Latin epitaph for the grave of his illustrious predecessor—an eloquent inscription, which concludes with the eloquent words, 'si monumentum quæris, circumspice.' He was employed to alter portions of Rochester Cathedral and Greenwich Hospital, and in Lichfield Street he built a house for the world-renowned anatomist and surgeon —the Scotsman, John Hunter.

The family of Mylnes may, in a certain sense, be described as hereditary master-masons to the Kings of Scotland, as the rhyming epitaph upon the family tomb in Old Greyfriars so quaintly puts it. The inscription begins with a Latin eulogy of 'John Milne,' in the course of which we read (translating) :—

'Robert, his brother's son, emulous of his virtues, as well as his successor in office, has, out of gratitude, erected this monument, such as it is, to his uncle. He died 24th December 1667 in the fifty-fifth year of his age.'

After this come the following curious rhyming lines in English :—

> 'Great artisan, grave senator, John Milne,
> Renowned for learning, prudence, parts, and skill,
> Who in his life Vitruvius' art had shown,
> Adorning others' monuments : his own
> Can have no other beauty than his name,
> His memory, and everlasting fame.
> Rare man he was, who could unite in one
> Highest and lowest occupation,
> To sit with statesmen, councillour to kings,
> To work with tradesmen in mechanick things,
> Majestic man, for person, wit, and grace
> This generation cannot fill his place.'

Near the ground we see :—

> 'Reader, John Milne, who maketh the fourth John,
> And, by descent from father unto son,
> Sixth master-mason to a royal race
> Of seven successive kings, sleeps in this place.

The Architect

Like the utterance of the friar's in 'The Jackdaw of Rheims,' this is somewhat 'regardless of grammar,' but we can often understand what we cannot parse.

The 'John Milne' to whom his nephew erected this monument, and who died in 1667, was the great-great-grandfather of the architect of St. Cecilia's. John Mylne had been master-mason to Charles I. and to Charles II., and for the latter monarch had drawn up plans for the Palace of Holyrood which were never executed. He, however, did much work in Scotland. In Edinburgh, he repaired the old crown-like steeple of St. Giles'; built 'Christ's Church at the Tron,' in the High Street; erected the fortifications at Leith; and, in what are now the gardens of Holyrood, executed a very beautiful sun-dial which exhibits 'C.R. & M.R.,' for Carolus Rex and (Henrietta) Maria Regina. In Forfarshire he built Panmure House for the second Earl of Panmure, and in Newcastle-on-Tyne erected the Church of St. Nicholas. John's brother, Alexander, a sculptor, was buried in the Chapel-Royal at Holyrood. In consequence of alterations prior to Queen Victoria's visit in 1850, this tomb came to be outside the limits of the Chapel as it now stands, but a large flat stone with a commemorative inscription was placed over the grave.

John Mylne, the tombstone states, was sixth master-mason to a royal race of seven successive kings. Can we corroborate this? The founder of the family was a John Mylne (1481), appointed master-mason to James III., and it was his son, Alexander, who filled the post in the court of James V. Thus, from James III. of Scotland to Charles II. of Great Britain there were *six* kings; but if we remember that it is John Mylne's nephew, Robert, who erects the tomb, and is speaking to the reader in the epitaph, we see that he is including his own service to James VII. and II., *i.e.* the seventh king from James III.

This Robert, the great-grandfather of the architect of St. Cecilia's, was a most important old Edinburgh builder or architect, for it was only in his time that the two offices began to be distinct. He served under Charles II., James II., William and Mary, and Queen Anne, and it was he who built the more modern portion of Holyrood Palace, of which Sir William Bruce of Kinross was architect. Upon the inner surface of one of the north-west pillars of the piazza of the quadrangle we can yet see, 'FVN. BE. RO. MILNE. M. M. I. JVL. 1671,' which, expanded, is read, 'Finished by Robert Mylne, Master-Mason, First July 1671.'

He also built, in 1690, to accommodate the rapidly increasing population, Mylne's Court on the north side of the Lawnmarket, and further down, on the same side in the High Street, Mylne's Square, lately demolished, in both of which localities resided for the next one hundred and fifty years some of the most ancient of our noble families. Mylne's Battery on the north-west corner of the Castle Rock, as well as the latest portion of the 'Royal Lodgings'—as they were always called—in the quadrangle of the Castle, were both erected by Robert Mylne in 1679. This same Mylne was the first man to enable pure water to be brought from the country into the city of Edinburgh. He constructed pipes from 'Tod's well at Comiston' which brought the water into several cisterns at various heights in the city, one of these being at the head of the Niddry Wynd.

The grandfather of Robert Mylne of St. Cecilia's, William Mylne of Leith, who died in 1728, and is also buried in Greyfriars', was architect and master-mason in the royal household, but his name does not seem to have been associated with any great work in Edinburgh. His son, however, Thomas Mylne of Powderhall (the father of our Robert), was a most active and notable Edinburgh character. He was the first to be styled 'Royal Architect,' and was surveyor to the city of Edinburgh.

He designed and built the old Royal Infirmary, in its day the worthy home of an ever-worthy charity, founded during the provostship of one of the most patriotic and far-sighted of Edinburgh's sons, Sir George

Drummond. A son of his, William, brother to Robert, has his name associated with a very important architectural feature of Edinburgh, viz. the old North Bridge, the foundation-stone of which was laid in 1763. William Mylne was likewise concerned in the construction of old Jamaica Street Bridge over the Clyde. It is curious that both of these bridges have been recently rebuilt, the new North Bridge of Edinburgh having been opened for traffic in September 1897, and the new Glasgow Bridge on May 24th, 1899. He settled in Dublin, where his greatest undertaking was the constructing of the waterworks, and he lies buried in St. Catherine's Church in that city. Thus St. Cecilia's Hall was designed by a man of no insignificant family, but the scion of a race inseparably bound up with the civic history and material progress of Scotland and her capital.

CHAPTER IV

THE PLAYERS AND THE SINGERS IN ST. CECILIA'S HALL

1. THE ORCHESTRA

The Professional Players.

QUITE the greatest amount of detailed information about the performers and singers in the hall in the Niddry Wynd is from the pen of old GEORGE THOMSON, the collector of the *Melodies of Scotland*, and a man intimately connected with the history of music in Scotland during the first three decades of this century.

He evidently wrote his recollections of the St. Cecilia concerts for the chapter dealing with that subject in Chambers's *Traditions of Edinburgh*, in which are to be found at least the *names* of many of the performers, singers, pieces played, and songs sung, as well as the names of those who comprised the audience, during the years in which Thomson played the violin in that long-forgotten orchestra. He is described by his contemporaries as 'an accomplished violinist.'

It is just possible that to-day, at the close of the

century,[1] we may have forgotten the great debt we owe to George Thomson for having collected, purified, edited, and adapted tunes to our Scots songs; for having laboured away at harmonising the tunes with the help of the great Germans—Beethoven, Haydn, Weber, Pleyel, Kozeluch, and Hummel; for having written and written again to composer and poet until these unbusinesslike geniuses were brought to complete their tasks and fulfil their promises. It is one thing for Genius to scatter her treasures broadcast, almost always without method, often with a touch of madness; but it means careful hard work and a respect for duty to recover these gems from amidst piles of old papers, the backs of letters or an occasional banknote, and, laboriously arranging them, fit them for public delectation.

George Thomson was a most indispensable person in our æsthetic history, the self-appointed honorary secretary to the Scottish Muses. Thomson is to us not only one of the most interesting, but one of the strongest, links with our artistic past. Born in 1757 at Limekilns in Fife, he became at seventeen years old a clerk in the office of a Writer to the Signet, and

---

[1] This was written two years before the publication of a life of Thomson—*George Thomson, the Friend of Burns: His Life and Correspondence.* By J. Cuthbert Hadden. London: J. C. Nimmo, 1898.

GEORGE THOMSON.
(*From Crombie's 'Men of Modern Athens.'*)

The Players and the Singers 55

some four or five years later, through the influence of no less well-known a literary celebrity than Home, the reverend author of *Douglas*, was appointed junior clerk to the Board of Trustees for Manufacturers for Scotland.

Wisely deciding not to allow ambition to make his life a time of fretful change and striving, he remained senior clerk to the Board throughout the whole of what some might call a totally uneventful professional career, yet one whose very placidity enabled Thomson to live, as it were, a parallel life full of artistic incident and interest.

'Having studied the violin, it was my custom,' he writes in a kind of autobiography, 'after the hours of business to con over our Scottish melodies, and to devour the choruses of Handel's oratorios, in which, when performed at St. Cecilia's Hall, I generally took a part along with a few other gentlemen,—Mr. Alexander Wight, one of the most eminent counsel at the bar, Mr. Gilbert Innes of Stow, Mr. John Russel, W.S., Mr. John Hutton, etc., it being then not uncommon for grave amateurs to assist at the Cecilia Concerts, one of the most interesting and liberal musical institutions that ever existed in Scotland or indeed in any country. I had so much delight in singing those matchless choruses and in practising the violin quartettes of Pleyel and Haydn, that it was with joy

I hailed the hour when, like the young amateur in the good old Scotch song, "I could hie me hame to my Cremona" and enjoy Haydn's admirable fancies.'

Here we have the true æstheticism, the love of the beautiful because it is beautiful, and for no other reason. We know how from 1792 to 1796, the year of Burns's death, Thomson was in constant correspondence with the poet about the 'magnum opus' for which Burns supplied in all one hundred and twenty songs, many of them original, others revisions and purifications. Such was one of the amateur violinists of the St. Cecilia orchestra, a man who has gone down to posterity as the friend and correspondent of Robert Burns, but a man who is also to be remembered as having wedded German harmony to Scottish pathos and who by his energy and perseverance in the cause of national art has deserved for all time coming the undying gratitude of each succeeding generation of Scotsmen.

Of Scottish songs Thomson published the following volumes :—

> Volume I. Songs the airs of which were all harmonised by Pleyel.
> Volume II. Songs the airs of which were all harmonised by Kozeluch.
> Volumes III. and IV. Songs the airs of which were all harmonised by Haydn.

The Players and the Singers

Volume v. Four airs harmonised by Haydn, twenty-six by Beethoven.

Volume vi. Contained fifty-two songs, twelve of which were harmonised by Haydn, thirteen by Beethoven, one by Kozeluch, twenty-one by Hogarth, and five by Sir Henry Bishop.

The first volume was published in 1793 and the sixth volume in 1841.

George Thomson died at Leith on February 18th, 1851, in his ninety-fourth year, but was buried in Kensal Green cemetery, London, where his wife had been laid ten years before.

Following Thomson's narrative, we read :—

'In the instrumental department we had Signor Puppo from Rome, or Naples, as leader and violin concerto player.'

GIUSEPPE (or JOSEPH) PUPPO was born at Lucca in 1749, and died in a hospital at Naples in 1827. Receiving his early musical education in Naples, and having studied the violin under Tartini, he made rapid progress and soon showed himself a brilliant performer. Thomson says of him—'Puppo charmed all hearers.' Like so many musicians, he had a chequered and wandering career, for between 1775 and 1784 he visited France, Spain, Portugal, England, Scotland, and Ireland, and was everywhere in great request as an accompanist, but never remained very long in one place, till he settled in Paris about 1789. Puppo may be described as an eccentric, dissatisfied man, evidently with great talents, but little power of effective self-direction. He appears to have been as long in Edinburgh as in any other place that he visited, for he was leader at St. Cecilia's from January 1778 to August 1782. He did not come to Edinburgh alone: 'Mrs. Puppo' came with him, and apparently also some relative—probably a brother of the name of Stefano, who advertises in the *Edinburgh Evening Courant* of June 24th, 1778, that he teaches languages at new lodgings in James's Court.

In July 1778 Signor and Signora Puppo were lodging in New Street, Canongate; earlier in the year they had been in lodgings 'facing the City Guard.' In March of the same year they have a curiously worded advertisement in the *Courant* to the effect that 'Mr. Puppo,' having been indisposed, is now ready to teach singing or playing on the harpsichord, and that 'Mrs. Puppo,' newly returned from London, where she had received lessons from Sacchini, is prepared to go to the country one day in the week. On July 24th, at a benefit concert for 'Mr. Fischer' in St. Cecilia's, Mrs. Puppo sang, and her husband and Schetky were instrumentalists.

In the *Edinburgh Evening Courant* of February 28th, 1778, a benefit concert for Mr. Puppo on March 2nd is advertised, 'when it is hoped he will receive the

The Players and the Singers 59

countenance from the public which his own merit besides his being first fiddle in the concert entitles him to.'

In February 1779, at a benefit concert for Schetky, a large gathering of professionals is recorded: 'Mrs. Melmoth, Mrs. Puppo, and Signor and Signora Corri' are all to sing, while Schetky, Reinagle, Clarke, and Puppo are to play.

On April 21st, in the same year, Puppo, Reinagle, and Corri take the leading instrumental parts at a concert after the play in the Theatre Royal.

On July 12th, Puppo announces that during the 'race week' he will give three morning concerts, at which, among other things, the overture was to be one of Lord Kelly's; Mrs. Corri was to sing 'The soldier tired of war's alarms,' Mrs. Puppo, 'For the lack of gold she's left me'; while Puppo and Reinagle were to play a 'duetto on tenor and violin,' Schetky a solo concerto on his 'cello, and Corri a rondo. Each concert 3s. 6d. to non-subscribers, *i.e.* to those not members of the Musical Society. It would seem as though at one time Puppo had not been 'going down,' as we would say, with the public, for the following appears on February 27th, 1779:[1] 'The Governors and Directors very earnestly recommend Mr. Puppo, whose concert is fixed for Tuesday, 9th March, to the counte-

[1] *Edinburgh Evening Courant*—twice repeated.

nance of the subscribers and of such ladies and gentlemen as frequent the weekly concert. The company may be assured that Mr. Puppo will do everything in his power to render the entertainment agreeable. Tickets 3s. each.'

In August, Mrs. Puppo announces that having gone to Musselburgh—no doubt for the holidays—she is to be found at Mrs. Christy's at Fisherrow, and is prepared to teach singing to ladies.

Puppo seems to have borne, by an almost inevitable pun, the nickname of 'Puppy,' as is seen below his portrait reproduced by the kind permission of Mr. Marr, to whose collection of musical curiosities the original belongs.

Puppo published very little music, and that was wholly instrumental. Though he died in a state of destitution and in a hospital to which he had been sent by the English musician, Professor Edward Taylor, Puppo might at one time have been called rich when he acted as *chef d'orchestre* at the Théâtre Français in 1799.

He is credited with saying smart things, only one of which has come down to us,—'Boccherini is the wife of Haydn.'

Thomson continues his list of performers thus:—
'Mr. Schetky from Germany, the principal violoncellist and a fine concerto player.'

SIGNOR PUPPY.
FIRST CATGUT SCRAPER
(*From a rare Print in the possession of Mr. Robert A. Marr, C.A.*)

Herr Schetky (or Schetki) has no niche in the temple of fame as arranged in Grove's *Dictionary of Musicians*, and any details of his life which exist are much scattered through out-of-the-way sources.

JOHANN GEORG CHRISTOFF SCHETKY was born at Hesse-Darmstadt in the year 1740, and died in Edinburgh, 29th November 1824, in the eighty-fourth year of his age.

His fourth son, John Christian, born in Ainslie's Close, Edinburgh, 11th August 1778, became marine painter in ordinary to George IV. and to her Majesty Queen Victoria. His life is written by his daughter —the granddaughter, therefore, of the old St. Cecilia Hall musician.

Young Schetky, like young Walter Scott, only once saw and was spoken to by Robert Burns in Edinburgh. Schetky the elder was dining with William Nicol and Allan Masterton, both High School masters, in the former's house, where Burns too was a guest. John and Charles Schetky, returning from a long day's truant-playing, passed the window, when they were espied by their father and master respectively. In the midst of the scolding, Nicol and Schetky were pushed right and left of the window by a burly, good-humoured countryman who threw the boys some 'bawbees for bannocks,' and told them to run off and be in time for the school next morning. The big man was Robert

Burns, and thus young Schetky saw them all, the three famous characters in

> 'Willie brewed a peck o' maut,
> And Rob and Allan cam to see.'

The facts in this life of J. C. Schetky must be taken as authoritative. The date of his arrival in Edinburgh in company with his younger brother Karl is there given as February 14th, 1773.

This statement as to the date cannot be verified from the contemporary Edinburgh newspapers.

In the *Edinburgh Evening Courant* of February 29th, 1772, there is the following intimation in two lines of the half column :—

'Yesterday arrived here Signor Schetki, principal violoncello to the Musical Society.'

This would make the date February 28th, 1772, a year earlier than the date given in the work before us, so that we must take it Schetky's granddaughter is here in error.

Schetky himself, twenty-six years after he came to Edinburgh, might well be excused if his recollection of the exact day of the month on which he arrived was not perfectly accurate. In the *Edinburgh Evening Courant* of January 17th, 1798, he inserts the following announcement: 'Mr. Schetky most respectfully informs his friends and the public that his concert (at Theatre

Royal) is fixed for the 9th of February next. Mr. Schetky begs leave to mention here that on the same day twenty-six years past he arrived in Edinburgh, since which time he has been honoured with the most generous patronage, and humbly hopes no part of his conduct has forfeited the same.' Tickets 3s. each at the music-shops and at his house in Foulis's Close. To begin at 7 P.M.

The father of J. G. C. Schetky was Louis Schetky,[1] secretary to the reigning Landgraf of Hesse-Darmstädt, a man whose duties were manifold, including everything from paying the household troops to playing at the court concerts. The family of Louis was large, and J. G. C. Schetky, the eldest, was intended for the profession of law, with which object he was sent to study in that faculty at the old university of the quaint little South German town of Jena.

It has not infrequently happened that many who have been sent to the study of law have had very little taste for it, and in a few cases they have providentially managed to break away from its dry-as-dust thraldom and indulge their natural aptitude for something else.

The 'something else' in the case of Schetky was music, a not altogether inexplicable tendency when we remember that 'his father before him' was musical.

[1] Descended from the Hungarian Barons von Teschky.

He soon became celebrated as a composer and 'celloist, and, while holding an appointment at the court of Hesse-Darmstadt, travelled for two years through Italy and France.

Amongst other royal persons he visited Stanislaus, the dethroned King of Poland, then residing at Luneville. He was here presented with the usual gold snuff-box, and advised to go on to Plombières and call on the two younger daughters of Louis Quinze of France, Mesdames Victoire and Adelaide.

Herr Schetky, acting on this excellent advice, found the Princesses playing the one on the harpsichord and the other on the violin.

Instead of hurrying off from Plombières, Schetky remained some little time, and wrote an air with variations for the Princesses, which they requested him later on to arrange as a duet for their harpsichord and violin.

On returning to Darmstadt, he and four other members of the court orchestra moved to Frankfort to form part of the imperial orchestra during the ceremonies in connection with the coronation of Joseph, King of the Romans, in the course of which he attracted royal notice by the excellence of his performance of a violoncello concerto of his own composition.

After the death of his patron, the Landgraf of Hesse, he commenced a journey to London *via* Flanders, where, at Lisle, he met Bremner—then the first music-publisher in London,—who had been commissioned by the musical world of Scotland to engage a first violoncellist for the St. Cecilia concerts in Edinburgh.

His last surviving daughter thus writes of her father's 'retirement' to Edinburgh :—

'Was it not strange that after being flattered and admired at foreign courts, and meeting with so much prosperity everywhere, he should at last settle down in a small place such as Edinburgh then was, in the remote country of Scotland! But I have sometimes imagined that this country then must have been more like an old Continental city than in its present state of progress. There were all the nobility of the country assembled from their ancient fastnesses in the north, the Courts of Law, the University, the little exiled court of France at Holyrood, where my father often appeared,[1] those splendid St. Cecilia concerts (the audience composed exclusively of the aristocracy), combining so much talent; add to this the easy access a well-educated and accomplished foreigner found to the best society—these things must, I think, have combined to make him like the place.'

J. G. C. Schetky's first friend in Edinburgh was not unnaturally the Hungarian, Joseph Reinagle, who had already been some time in Edinburgh when Schetky arrived, and whose daughter, his eldest, Maria Anna Theresa, we are not very surprised to hear Schetky married in 1774.

[1] Herr Schetky used to play at the private concerts given by the banished Princes, afterwards Louis XVIII. and Charles X., during their residence at Holyrood Palace after the Revolution of 1793.

The ceremony took place in the old Episcopal Chapel in the Cowgate, now St. Patrick's. They set up house in Ainslie's Close, but a few years later removed to Foulis's Close, High Street, where eleven of their children were born, all of whom were baptized in the old chapel just mentioned: of these children seven grew up.

In the Edinburgh Directory of to-day may still be found South Foulis Close, but it is not probable that the house in which the Schetkys lived for twenty-one years could be identified: it was very dilapidated in 1863, and since that date two strong spirits, of destruction and reconstruction respectively, have been abroad in the High Street.

In February 1769, Schetky states in the *Edinburgh Evening Courant* that his lodgings are in 'Miln's Court.'

The old *Dictionary of Musicians*[1] thus disposes of 'J. G. C. Schetky, an excellent violoncellist, in the service of the Prince of Hesse-Darmstadt in 1772. Previously to the year 1780, he had published in London and at the Hague five operas of instrumental music. He has also left at his death many manuscript compositions for his instrument. He died at Edinburgh in 1773.'

The 'died' here must be a printer's error for 'arrived.'

[1] London, 1824.

We are able, through the kindness of Mr. James G. Ferguson, to publish for the first time the entry of the interment of this, in his day, most important musician, who spent forty-nine years of his life in Edinburgh.

'Extracted from the Records of Burials in the Canongate Burying-ground, by James G. Ferguson, Recorder of City Burying-grounds.

'1824.—SCHETKY. Mr. John George Christopher Schetky, native of Darmstadt, Upper Rhine; for many years Professor of Music in Edinburgh, died 29th ult:[1] interred in the west side six feet north-west of Sharp's ground, and four feet south-west of Langley's stone. . . . Old age.'

We may now trace Schetky here and there through Old Edinburgh. In the first place, we find him reported by Burns to have been drinking with him, and to have composed a tune for one of his songs. The allusion occurs in a postscript to a Clarinda letter, dated 'Thursday morning 24th January' (1788), and runs thus:—

'*Evening*, 9 *o'clock*.—I am here absolutely unfit to finish my letter, pretty hearty after a bowl which has been constantly plied since dinner till this moment. I have been with Mr. Schetky the musician, and he has set it finely. I have no distinct ideas of anything, but that I have drunk your health twice to-night, and that you are all my soul holds dear in this world.'

The 'it' of which Schetky was the musical father was that lovely song of Burns's, 'Clarinda, mistress of my

---

[1] Died 29th November, and buried on 3rd December.

soul,' than which surely no sadder lament was ever penned :—

> 'Clarinda, mistress of my soul,
>   The measured time is run !
> The wretch beneath the dreary pole
>   So marks his latest sun.
>
> We part—but by those precious drops
>   That fill thy lovely eyes,
> No other light shall guide my steps
>   Till thy bright beams arise.
>
> She, the fair sun of all her sex,
>   Has blest my glorious day :
> And shall a glimmering planet fix
>   My worship to its ray?'

The poet at this time contemplated an early departure from Edinburgh.

Schetky, some believe, composed another Scots tune, the newer air to 'Mary's Dream'; for Stenhouse in his *Lyric Poetry and Music of Scotland*[1] thus writes:—'The second set of the air to Lowe's song is, I believe, the composition of my friend Mr. Schetky, the celebrated violoncello player in Edinburgh.'[2]

The evening of the hard drinking in the old Lawnmarket house was not the first occasion on which Burns and Schetky had been in the same room

---

[1] Page 40, 1853 edition.
[2] Mr. John Glen says that Stenhouse is mistaken in attributing this air to Schetky.

J. G. C. SCHETKY.

(From Stewart Watson's picture of 'The Inauguration of Robert Burns as Poet-Laureate of the Lodge Canongate Kilwinning No. 2.')

together, for, according to the well-known picture by Stewart Watson of the interior of St. John's Chapel, Canongate, on the evening of the 'Inauguration of Robert Burns as Poet-Laureate of the Canongate Kilwinning Lodge No. 2, 1787,' J. G. C. Schetky is there, and with his 'cello, too. He was, in fact, 'Brother Schetky' of this Lodge of Freemasons, and is the figure to the extreme right, and the highest of the group against the organ. That old organ is still in the hall of the Canongate Kilwinning Lodge—indeed, the old hall is very much as Burns and Schetky last saw it: it teems with Old Edinburgh memories.

From a small and now very rare book entitled *A Winter with Robert Burns*,[1] which is virtually an account of each of the persons represented in this important picture of Edinburgh Freemasons, we feel justified in quoting the little that is said of this musician:—'No. 35, J. G. C. Schetky, Music Teacher, Fowles' Close, Fountain Well.

> 'Nae *lente largo* in the play,
> But *allegretto forte* gay
> Harmonious flows.—BURNS.

'Schetky, a distinguished musician, was the father of the eminent sketcher and marine painter to George IV. He was by birth a German, and came to Edinburgh about the middle of last century. He was at this

[1] Printed by Peter Brown, James' Square, Edinburgh, 1846.

period employed in the St. Cecilia Hall, where the weekly concerts during the winter months were attended by all the rank, beauty, and fashion of Edinburgh. He composed the *March of the Defensive Band*, which Mr. Crosbie, W.S. (the first master of that lodge), commanded. It is needless to remark that it was not Burns who wrote to it:

' " Colonel Crosbie takes the field,
  To France and Spain he will not yield,
  But still maintains his high command
  At the head of the Noble Defensive Band."

'Schetky's howff was *Hogg's* tavern, where he constituted the Boar Club, each *Bore* contributing a halfpenny to the *Pig*, and Mr. Aldridge, a brother-musician, being perpetual Grand Grunter of the Sty. Burns got Schetky to compose an air to his "Clarinda, mistress of my soul."

'He is represented in the picture with his instrument, the violoncello, on which he excelled in concertos.'

Schetky was evidently very much at home in 'Auld Reekie,' with whose facility for deep and frequent potations his Teutonic soul would be in full sympathy. He was one of the *original* members of the 'Boar Club,' founded in 1787—one of those many eccentric, convivial 'clubs' of Old Edinburgh. They were all, in truth, societies for drinking: one differed from another merely in the particular excuse alleged for the drinking. The Boar's Club place of meeting was, of course, in a tavern—Daniel Hogg's, in Shakespeare Square; and Schetky was 'deputy-grand-boar,' whatever that meant. The name of the club had of course reference to 'mine host's.'

'Brother Schetky' had a warlike spirit on behalf of the land of his adoption, for he composed a march for the Royal Edinburgh Volunteers, the company to which he belonged.

On yet one more historic occasion does the ubiquitous Schetky appear, viz., at the laying of the foundation-stone of the present buildings of the University of Edinburgh, when he led a band of singers who, in the procession, walked between the students and the various Lodges of Freemasons represented.

The stone was laid with full Masonic honours on the 16th September 1789, by the Right Hon. Lord Napier of Merchistoun, Grand Master-Mason of Scotland; so that if Schetky's ghost were ever to reappear in the 'Quad,' and were to overhear an inaccurate tourist assigning a wrong date to the classic fabric, he could say with Edie Ochiltree, 'I mind the biggin' o't.' The notices of Schetky and his concerts—benefits and otherwise—in old Edinburgh newspapers are quite too numerous to mention, which is not remarkable, considering the long time he lived in Edinburgh.

But Edinburgh actually very nearly missed possessing Schetky altogether, for it is said that, on arriving at Ramsay's Inn near the Cowgate Port, he was so poorly impressed with the city, had his ears so loudly assailed by her cries, and his nose by her odours, that he almost determined to be off. Probably his thirst detained him.

Next on Thomson's list we have—

'JOSEPH REINAGLE, a clever violoncello and viola player.' Reinagle does not obtain elaborate treatment in the pages of Grove, from which we learn that he was born at Portsmouth, but the date neither of his birth (1762) nor his death (1836) is given. Reinagle was of Austrian descent; his father, Joseph Reinagle, having served in the Hungarian army under the Empress Maria Theresa, and having come to Scotland with the 'Old Pretender' in 1715.

Old Reinagle had intended his son to enter the navy, possibly for no other reason than that he was born at Portsmouth; 'but,' says the *Dictionary of Musicians*,[1] 'that idea being abandoned, he was removed to Edinburgh.' We are sure Edinburgh benefited by the move, but it is by no means apparent why the only alternative, after abandoning the idea of entering the navy, was to enter Edinburgh.

Joseph Reinagle, senior, it seems, obtained through

[1] London, 1824.

the influence of Lord Kelly the post of 'Trumpeter to the King.' Through the courtesy of the Queen's and Lord Treasurer's Remembrancer a search made in the records of the Exchequer Office has revealed the fact that, as reckoned from the time at which his salary began, Joseph Reinagle was appointed to be trumpeter on 21st May 1762. Joseph Reinagle, junior, was made to study under parental guidance the French horn and trumpet. It was not long before Joseph appeared in public as concerto player on both these instruments, but, upon medical advice, gave them up and began to study the violoncello with Schetky as his teacher. Owing to his brother Hugh's growing fame as a 'celloist, Joseph relinquished his instrument, and proceeded under Aragoni and Pinto[1] to master the viola. It would also appear that Reinagle studied the harpsichord, for at a concert in April 1770 for 'Mr. and Mrs. Taylor,' a 'sonata on the harpsichord by Mr. Reinagle, a scholar of Mr. Taylor's,' is announced.

In course of time 'he was appointed,' says the old *Dictionary*, 'leader of the concerts at the theatre in Edinburgh.' To arrive at the truth we must delete the words 'at the theatre': the concert in Edinburgh alluded to is that at St. Cecilia's.

[1] This latter violinist, born of Italian parents in London, died in 1773. Both musicians resided for some time in Edinburgh.

His brother Hugh having died at Lisbon, Joseph felt free to resume the 'cello, which was thenceforth his instrument to the time of his death. He, too, has left his name scattered throughout the Edinburgh newspapers of his time.

In February 1779 he plays his 'cello at a benefit concert of Schetky's; on 6th April, at St. Cecilia's, he and M'Glashan have a joint benefit: in the same month he and Puppo play at more than one concert 'between two acts of the Play' at the 'Theatre Royal'; and there is no doubt that Reinagle helped his friend Puppo with his venture of those 'morning concerts' in 1779.

In 1779, Reinagle was living at the foot of Blackfriars' Wynd; in 1785, at Morrison's Close, scale stairs.

We next hear of him playing in concertos with Cramer and others in London, after two years' sojourn in Dublin, where he had gone in 1785, on the invitation of Lord Westmoreland, the Lord Lieutenant.

He returned to London and played at Salomon's concerts as principal 'celloist during the time that Haydn conducted them. Haydn was in London in 1790, and again in 1794.

By 1821 Reinagle had gone to Oxford, for he writes to Nathaniel Gow from there. He had been well received in the old city some years previously when he went to play at the Oxford concerts, and on the advice of Lord Abingdon he settled there, where he died in 1836.

Reinagle published five works, and left behind him a quantity of MSS.—overtures, trios and duets for violins and pianoforte. One of his works is *A Treatise on the Violoncello.* Joseph Reinagle, senior, married a Scotswoman—Annie Laurie—and their daughter, Maria Anna Theresa, Mrs. J. G. C. Schetky, is thus described by her daughter [1]:—

'My mother was a highly accomplished artist in both painting and music, having a splendid voice. She painted in various styles, but miniature-painting was her forte. How excellent she was in all respects, a perfect lady in manner and goodness and piety—such a wife and mother in devotedness, and so beloved and respected! I was never so happy as by her side.' [2]

J. G. C. Schetky thus married the daughter of Joseph Reinagle the elder, and sister of Joseph Reinagle the younger.

Thomson's list proceeds:—

'Mr. Barnard, a very elegant violinist.' MR. BARNARD is, we fear, almost unknown to posthumous fame, whatever he might have been to contemporary. Mr.

---

[1] *Life of John Christian Schetky*, page 100.
[2] *Edinburgh Evening Courant*, Nov. 12th, 1785.—'Mrs. Schetky continues to teach drawing and painting at her lodgings, Foulis's Close.'

Barnard is mentioned in a concert given in St. Cecilia's on December 8th, 1779, for at a benefit on behalf of Mrs. Marchetti 'a clarinet concerto by Mr. Barnard' is announced.

Thomson continues :—' The most accomplished violin-player I ever heard, Paganini only excepted—I mean Giornovicki, who possessed in a most extraordinary degree the various requisites of his beautiful art; execution particularly brilliant and finely articulated as possible, a tone of the richest and most exquisite quality, expression of the utmost delicacy, grace, and tenderness, and an animation that commanded your most intense and eager attention. Paganini did not appear in Edinburgh till thirty years after the hall was closed' (it was closed in 1800 : Paganini played in Edinburgh in 1831). 'There, as well as at private parties, I heard Giornovicki often, and always with no less delight than I listened to Paganini. Both, if I may use the expression, threw their whole hearts and souls into their Cremonas, bows, and fingers.' This is indeed high praise; but one who heard Paganini, the acknowledged king of violinists, ought to have been able to judge. We have known one person who heard Paganini play—an old lady who died in 1897, aged eighty-one; as a girl she had heard Paganini in the Music Hall in George Street.

GIOVANNI MARIE GIORNOVICHJ, as he is known to

have signed his name, but sometimes styled in England John M. Giornovicki, Jarnowick, or even Jornelli, was born at Palermo in 1745, and died at St. Petersburg in 1804. A pupil both in 'music and morals' of the somewhat famous and rather notorious Lolli, Giornovicki made his *début* in Paris in 1770, where, having played a concerto of his master's which did not 'take,' he substituted for it 'a thing of his own composing' which did.

Domenico Dragonetti, one of the greatest double-bass players of his day, is said to have declared of Giornovicki that his violin-playing was the most elegant and graceful he had ever heard previously to Paganini's, but that perhaps it lacked power. George Hogarth writes of his performance thus:—'Jarnowick was but a slender musician. His concertos are agreeable and brilliant, but destitute of profundity and grandeur. His performance was graceful and elegant, and his tone was pure.'

Hogarth, an Edinburgh man,[1] presumably heard Giornovicki during his Edinburgh visit, which was not earlier than 1796 nor later than 1801.

The latter date is fixed rather curiously thus: there is in the possession of Mr. John Glen a copy of 'Mr. Jarnovichi's Reel,' published by Gow and Shepherd, 41 North Bridge Street. This firm removed to Princes Street in 1801. We have heard Mr. Glen play the

[1] Father-in-law of Charles Dickens.

opening bars of the reel, sufficient to show that this Italian had very successfully imitated the Scottish style of dance music.

On May 4th, 1791, Giornovicki gave his first London concert—then as now a great event in the musical life of any professional. Gifted as this Sicilian was, he was both insolent and conceited, and as a natural result was for ever offending and quarrelling with people. On one occasion it is related that he so far forgot himself as to strike the Chevalier St. George, himself both a violinist and a swordsman, whereupon the Prince, instead of challenging him, merely said, 'I have too much regard for his musical talent to fight him.' More serious was a quarrel with J. B. Cramer, which resulted in Giornovicki being called out to a duel. We do not know how it ended, but Giornovicki is said to have been a good swordsman. His death in St. Petersburg took place quite suddenly in 1804.

From Parke's *Musical Memoirs*,[1] which cover the interval from 1784 to 1830, we glean some further but merely gossipy information about this musician. W. T. Parke, who was for forty years principal oboist to the Theatre Royal, Covent Garden, under date March 12th, 1793, writes thus of a performance in the 'new Theatre Royal, Drury Lane':—'At the end of the second act, a concerto was performed on the violin by

[1] London, 1830.

Mr. Jarnovicki. Jarnovicki displayed a fine round and sweet tone; his execution was brilliant, and his style natural and pleasing. His concerto, though difficult, was full of melody, and he played it with great ease. He was generally and vehemently applauded.'

Further on[1] we read:—'His Royal Highness the Duke of York gave a grand concert of instrumental music at York House, Piccadilly, at which their Majesties and the Princesses were present. . . . Jarnovicki was to have played a concerto on the violin, by desire of her Majesty, who had never heard him perform, but on coming into the room just before the music commenced, and perceiving Salomon there (to whom he bore a violent hatred), Jarnovicki vented his spleen by leaving the house immediately. This insolent foreigner, who suffered professional jealousy to supersede the respect due to the Queen of a great nation, deserved punishment for his presumption.'

Jarnovicki once wanted to call a coach in Tottenham Court Road, and although he had been in London for several years (since 1789), he could not summon up enough English to direct the driver to his house. At last he exclaimed, ' Malbrouk s'en va-t-en guerre,' which enabled the bystanders to guess that he meant Marlborough Street.[2]

Parke gives us a few details about this man.[3] ' Jar-

[1] *Musical Memoirs*, vol. i. p. 196.   [2] *Ibid.* p. 274.
[3] *Ibid.* p. 338.

novicki, that musical Hotspur, died at St. Petersburg in the year 1804, of apoplexy. He was an accomplished violin player, and his music is melodious and pleasing. He was not, however, a profound musician, as he merely wrote the subjects and solo parts of his concertos, and employed an abler theorist than himself to harmonise them. Jarnovicki was highly patronised while in England, but his violent disposition disgusted most of his supporters.' Parke tells us that George IV., when Prince of Wales, learned the violoncello under John Crosdill, and that at the Prince's musical parties Jarnovicki was sometimes present.

The next performer we shall notice is HIERONYMUS or HIERONYMO or GIROLAMO[1] STABILINI—another name not to be found in Grove. He appears to have succeeded Puppo in 1783, Puppo having resigned in the previous year, as leader and first violin in the St. Cecilia's orchestra, which post he held till the concerts were given up.

In *Kay's Portraits*,[2] on the plate for page 293, we have a portrait of this man along with four others: Stabilini's is the right upper one of the set. The letterpress says of it:—' A capital resemblance of an Italian musician, Hieronymo Stabilini, who was a native of Rome and came to Edinburgh about the year 1778. The musical talents of Stabilini were much admired,

[1] The English form of this name is ' Jerome.'   [2] Vol. i.

SIGNOR STABILINI, VIOLINIST.
(*From 'Kay's Portraits.'*)

The Players and the Singers 87

and although, unlike the modern Orpheus, Paganini, he could not "discourse sweet airs" from a single piece of catgut, his performances on the four pieces were generally admired.' The date of Stabilini's arrival in Edinburgh was 1783, although it was not until the following year that his name appeared on a St. Cecilia concert programme.

It appears that Stabilini, who was no horseman, was unfortunate enough to injure his 'bow arm' on one occasion at Leith races, after which accident it was remarked that he never played quite so well as before.

George Thomson evidently did not think quite so highly of Stabilini's technique as the writer in *Kay's Portraits*, for he says of him:—'He had a good round tone, though to my apprehension he did not exceed mediocrity as a performer.'

Stabilini figures in Stewart Watson's picture, 'The Inauguration of Robert Burns as Poet-Laureate of the Lodge Canongate Kilwinning No. 2.' He is the second figure from the extreme left in front of the organ, as will be seen from the portion of the picture reproduced on page 139. To quote again from *A Winter with Burns*, we find the following slight notice of 'No. 27, Signor Stabilini, North Bridge.

'To give them music was his charge.—BURNS.

'Signor Stabilini, an Italian, was a celebrated player

on the violin, and during this winter was giving weekly concerts in Edinburgh of vocal and instrumental music in conjunction with Signors Urbani, Torrigiani, Corri, and others. Burns writes more than once in reference to his attendance at those concerts:—" The members of the lodge, on account of the prevalent predilection for music, induced the attendance and services of the first professional talent which the city could command.'" It will be noticed that the line from Burns given above was the one intended in 'Tam o' Shanter' to apply to the devil,—there are those who would not disapprove of the extension of the application.

Stabilini was a member of the Royal Edinburgh Volunteers, his name appearing not far from Schetky's in a printed roll of the corps. Mr. John Glen has a copy of this exceedingly rare book.

Stabilini was no blind admirer of Corelli, for it is recorded that on being asked at supper, after a concert at which certain of that composer's trios had been much applauded, what sort of music they had been having, he replied:

> 'A piece av toarky for a hungree bellee
> Is moatch supeerior to Corelli.'

Stabilini was, to put it mildly, a *bon vivant*; Chambers describes him as 'broken down by dissipation.' The following is told of him in *Kay's Portraits*:[1]

[1] Vol. i.

'Stabilini was particularly intimate with Corri, a countryman of his own and teacher of eminence, who built the music-rooms called the Adelphi Theatre at the head of Broughton Street. One evening he and Corri had sat down for a convivial time, having provided themselves with Scotch whisky in place of the light wines of their own country, with the result that evening became night and night the "small hours" before either was aware of it. At last Stabilini rose, and opening a shutter exclaimed, "Corri, Corri, begar, it's to-morrow!"' From this we see that to-morrow comes only to those who don't know day from night.

Stabilini has left many traces of himself in contemporary periodical literature.

On February 17th, 1785, Stabilini had a benefit concert in St. Cecilia's Hall; in June he played the first violin at a concert of Mr. Aitkin's in Dunn's Assembly Rooms, and in July in the same place he and Corri gave a joint concert.

In Stark's *Picture of Edinburgh*[1] we have the following account of Stabilini's arrival in Edinburgh: 'After Puppo had withdrawn himself from the weekly concerts, the Directors were at no small pains to get a proper person to supply his place as the leader of the orchestra. At this time a young performer of promising celebrity as a violin player appeared at Rome,

[1] 1806.

and the Directors resolved to invite him to settle in the Scottish capital. The offer was accepted, and Signor Stabilini arrived at Edinburgh in the year 1783. The performer made his first essay in such a style as to gain unqualified approbation, and he was declared not unworthy to succeed his celebrated predecessor. But Signor Stabilini, though a respectable performer, probably from the want of rivalship in his department, has never advanced beyond the limits to which his talents had already arrived. He, however, still continues a favourite with the public, and though better performers sometimes visit the metropolis, he is still to be considered as the first resident violin player in Edinburgh.'

This is qualified praise, but it is interesting as having been written while the subject of it was still alive. In 1787 Stabilini's house was in 6 Shakespeare Square. In 1790 Stabilini was living in a house at the north side of St. James's Square; six years later in North St. James's Street. In the year 1790 he and Schetky produced at the Theatre Royal 'a superb pantomimic spectacle': Schetky wrote the music, Stabilini conducted.

This musician is said to have been a great favourite of Mr. Skene of Skene. He died at Edinburgh, and was buried in the graveyard of St. Cuthbert's or the 'West Kirk.' The tombstone may be seen to this day, built into the old wall that skirts the ground on

The Players and the Singers 91

the right of the path leading from the main or west entrance. The stone is surmounted by a lyre, below which is written 'Muta Jacet,' and it bears the following inscription :—'Memoriæ Hieronymi Stabilini; amici mœrentes posuerunt. Romæ natus; Edinæ obiit; Mens. Jul. MDCCCXV. Ætat LIV.'

By the kindness of Mr. Ferguson of the Record Office (City Chambers, Edinburgh), we are able to give the entry of the interment of Stabilini's remains :—

'*July* 1815.—West Kirk. Mortality Ledger. Stabelino, 16th, Greitoni Stabelino from Rose Street. On shoulders. An Italian Musician; lys 6 ft. N. Glespie's[1] trough stone. Age 53. Dropsy.'

We can picture the scene so well: the poor foreign musician dying of dropsy in his humble lodgings in Rose Street—so emphatically even at that time a 'back street,' whichever way you take it—and then carried out 'feet foremost,' as the saying is, on the shoulders of one or two friends, presumably his late boon-companions, to be laid in that historic old churchyard, and then—forgotten. Fifty-three years separate 'Romæ natus' from 'Edinæ obiit.'

The *Scots Magazine* for 1815 contains the following in its obituary :—

'13*th July* 1815.—At Edinburgh, Gerolamo Stabilini, a native of Rome, for twenty-three years past well-known as

---
[1] Gillespie's (?)

the leader of the Edinburgh Concerts. This performer's execution as well as his expression, particularly as an adagio player on the violin, have been seldom equalled, and his loss will long be remembered with regret by the admirers of music in this metropolis.'

The following occurs in Stenhouse's *Lyric Poetry and Music of Scotland*, 1853, as a note on the song, 'I'll aye ca' in by yon town':—'The fine old air called "I'll gang nae mair to yon town," which was the first line of an old ballad. . . . The tune appears in Oswald's *Caledonian Pocket Companion*. . . . This air was introduced as a rondo with variations in a violin concerto composed by the late Mr. Giralamo Stabilini, and performed by him at Edinburgh with great applause.'

The editor of 'Paterson's Edition' of the *Poems of Robert Burns* is responsible for the following:[1]—'It may interest some readers to be told that the air was a marked favourite of King George IV.' (The air alluded to is 'I'll gang nae mair to yon town.')

'Signor Girolamo Stabilini introduced it as a rondo with variations in a violin concerto which was performed between the play *Rob Roy* and the after-piece on the occasion of his Majesty attending the Theatre of Edinburgh in 1822, and it was observed that the

[1] Mr. John Glen alleges that this information is due to Nathaniel Gow.

W. CRAMER.

(*From an Engraving in the British Museum after the painting by T. Hardy.*)

King drummed with his fingers to the music while sitting in his box.'

Dalzell,[1] speaking of violins made by Guarnerius, says: 'Stradivarius had been long the maker in highest repute, but now Joseph Guarnerius begins to rival him, and some even gave his instruments the preference. One of superior quality, the workmanship of this latter artist, made in 1732, was brought from Rome in 1783 or 1784 by Girolamo Stabilini, the last leader of the Gentlemen's Concert in St. Cecilia's Hall which subsisted long in the northern metropolis.'

WILHELM CRAMER, or the 'elder Cramer,' was born at Manheim about 1730 (some give 1745), and died in London in 1805 (some give 1799). He was the father of a much better-known man, Johann Baptist Cramer, but both were excellent violinists. It is with the elder Cramer that we are concerned in the history of St. Cecilia's, although he was accompanied on his first visit to Edinburgh by his son Johann,[2] 'even then a wonderful pianist.'[3] Later, we are told, '*their* assistance was anxiously sought for in every orchestra of importance throughout the kingdom.'

Just as Reinagle had hospitably received Schetky as a stranger from Germany, so we are told did the Schetkys in their turn entertain the Cramers on their musical tour through England and Scotland.

[1] *Memoirs of Music in Scotland.*   [2] Born 1771, died 1858.
[3] *Life of J. C. Schetky*, p. 13.

'When John (*i.e.* J. C. Schetky) was about six years old (1784 or 1785) . . . Mr. and Mrs. Cramer came from Germany, bringing their son John (afterwards the celebrated composer and even at that time a wonderful pianist), on a musical tour through England and Scotland; and on reaching Edinburgh were received by my grandfather with his accustomed hospitality.'[1]

J. B. Cramer was indeed one of the indispensable conditions of the success of a fashionable concert in London between 1790 and 1830: he was great as a violinist and great as a conductor both at concert, opera, and oratorio. He had the *entrée* of all the houses of the aristocratic patrons of music, including the Prince Regent's.

The father had, however, no mean career: in 1784 and in 1787 he led the violins at the Handel Festival in Westminster Abbey. Thomson writes of a visit of his to Edinburgh:—

'When the celebrated leader, the elder Cramer, visited St. Cecilia's Hall and played a charming spirited overture of Haydn's, an old amateur next to whom I was seated, asked me: "Whose music is that now?" "Haydn's, sir," said I. "Poor new-fangled stuff!" he replied. "I hope I shall never hear it again."'

The *Edinburgh Evening Courant* of July 30th, 1785,

[1] *Life of J. C. Schetky*, p. 13.

J. B. CRAMER.
(From a Print in the British Museum after the Original Picture by J. Pocock.)

The Players and the Singers

has the following interesting paragraph:—'At the oratorio of "Samson" last night at St. Cecilia's Hall, Mr. Cramer, the leader at the commemoration of Handel, conducted the orchestra with his usual ability.' . . . 'Young Mr. Cramer on the pianoforte was most deservedly admired.' Tenducci sang at this concert. 'Mr. Cramer's benefit on Tuesday next' is a further announcement: this alludes to a concert which was announced on August 1st, 1785, to be postponed on account of an appearance of Mrs. Siddons at the Theatre Royal. This brings the time and the manner of the time vividly before us: 'mutual accommodation' was the excellent plan adopted here,—it was also a most wise one, for it was not to be expected that Cramer would have had many at St. Cecilia's on the same night that Siddons was declaiming in Shakespeare Square.

Franz or François Cramer was the second son of Wilhelm Cramer; he was born at Schwetzingen, near Manheim, in 1772. He also was a famous 'leader of the band' in London.

Thomson's list concludes with 'Stephen Clarke, an excellent organist and harpsichord player, and twelve or fifteen violins, basses, flutes, violas, horns, and clarionets, with extra performers often from London.' 'From London'—quite as in our own day: London is called in when anything very special is wanted.

STEPHEN CLARKE, however, represented in excellent style the native school of composers, and was concerned in no insignificant way in furnishing airs for the various collections of Scots songs for which Burns wrote so much. He was most serviceable to Burns and his collectors, not only in composing airs, but in 'taking down' tunes while they were being sung or whistled.

Clarke was a teacher of music in Edinburgh, and also organist to the 'Episcopal Chapel in the Cowgate,' Old St. Paul's in South Gray's Close, now St. Patrick's Roman Catholic Church. In 1785 he was living in Gosford's Close, Lawnmarket. Clarke died in Edinburgh, August 6th, 1797, and was succeeded by his son William, who harmonised some of his father's tunes for Johnson's *Musical Museum*, but was very much less talented.

The origin of the tune, 'Ca' the yowes to the knowes,' is interesting. Burns says :—'I am flattered at your adopting "Ca' the yowes to the knowes," as it was owing to me that it ever saw the light. About seven years ago I was well acquainted with a worthy little fellow of a clergyman, a Mr. Clunie, who sang it charmingly then, and, at my request, Mr. Clarke took it down from his singing.'

Again, as to 'Ye banks and braes o' bonnie Doon' he writes :—'This air, I think, might find a place

The Players and the Singers 101

among your hundred. . . . Do you know the history of the air? It is curious enough. A good many years ago, Mr. James Miller, writer in your good town, a gentleman whom possibly you know, was in company with our friend Clarke, and, talking of Scottish music, Miller expressed an ardent ambition to be able to compose a Scots air. Mr. Clarke, partly by way of joke, told him to keep to the black keys of the harpsichord, and preserve some kind of rhythm, and he would infallibly compose a Scots air. Certain it is that in a few days Mr. Miller produced the rudiments of an air which Mr. Clarke with some touches and corrections fashioned into the tune in question. . . . This account which I have just given you, Mr. Clarke informed me of several years ago.'

'Mr. Clarke' is frequently mentioned in the Burns-Thomson letters. Thus in the seventh (7th April 1793) Burns writes :—'"Craigieburn Wood," in the opinion of Mr. Clarke, is one of our sweetest Scottish songs. He is quite an enthusiast about it; and I would take his taste for Scottish music against the taste of most connoisseurs.'

Again in letter xiii. (September 1793), writing of the 'Scots wha hae' air, he says :—'Clarke's set of the tune, with his bass, you will find in the *Museum*; though I am afraid that the air is not what will entitle it to a place in your elegant selection.'

Again Burns writes of Clarke, 'You know his taste is a standard.' In letters xvii., xviii., xx., and xxv. this musician is further mentioned.

Clarke 'took down' the tune put to Burns's song, 'What will I do gin my hoggie die?' from an old woman's singing it while spinning outside her cottage in a hamlet of Liddesdale.[1] In the same way he preserved the air to an old ballad, 'Our guidman came hame at e'en,' while it was being sung by an old man of the name of Geikie, a barber in the Candlemaker Row in Edinburgh.

Clarke composed several Scottish tunes. Stenhouse in his *Lyric Poetry and Music of Scotland*,[2] writes:— 'In the *Museum*, the ballad of "William and Margaret" by Mr. Hallet is adapted to a beautiful slow melody which was composed by the late Mr. Stephen Clarke of Edinburgh, organist.'[3]

Again,[4] speaking of the anonymous song, 'Chanticleer wi' noisy whistle,' he says:—'The words are adapted to a fine melody which was composed by the late Mr. Stephen Clarke.'[3]

Once more, it appears that Clarke composed the tune for Burns's patriotic song, 'Does haughty Gaul

---

[1] As to this statement Mr. John Glen remarks:—'Tune published before Burns knew Clarke.'
[2] Page 472.   [3] 'Not in the Scottish style' (Glen).
[4] *Ibid.* p. 481.

STEPHEN CLARKE, ORGANIST.
(From Stewart Watson's picture of 'The Inauguration of Robert Burns as Poet-Laureate of the Lodge Canongate Kilwinning No. 2.')

invasion threat?' written in 1795. The song with Clarke's music was distributed amongst the Dumfries Volunteers, the corps of which Burns was a member. Burns calls it his 'Volunteer Ballad,' and says:—'Our friend Clarke has indeed done well. I have not met with anything that has pleased me so much.'[1]

Burns relied very much on Clarke's critical judgment: having written the song, 'Here's to thy health, my bonnie lass,' for Johnson's *Museum*, he submits two tunes for it, asking Clarke to adopt whichever he likes best.

It is always interesting to know a man's favourite tune—especially a composer's. Clarke's was the tune, 'The Braes of Balquhidder.' Clarke wrote below the song set to it—'And I'll kiss thee yet'—'I am charmed with this song almost as much as the lover is with "Bonnie Peggy Alison."—S. C.'

It was to gratify Stephen Clarke that Burns wrote the very pretty song, 'Phillis the Queen o' the Fair.' The heroine of it had a name in itself almost enough to annihilate the very first strivings towards articulation of the most fervent poetical spirit that ever burned in a male breast—Miss Philadelphia MacMurdo.

In the painting of Burns's installation as poet-laureate of the Canongate Kilwinning Lodge, No. 33 in the musician group is named 'Samuel Clarke,

[1] 'Quite a martial tune' (Mr. John Glen).

organist of Cowgate Chapel.' This is clearly a mistake for Stephen Clarke, who was, as we have seen, a contemporary of Burns and also organist of the Cowgate Chapel.

In 1790 Clarke was living at 6 Canal Street.

The Professional Orchestra Proper.

After so great a lapse of time it is a matter of considerable difficulty to discover the names of the men who made up the 'rank and file' of that old St. Cecilia Orchestra; but the first Directory of Edinburgh ever published ought to prove something more than a broken reed.

It was published in 1774, and the following is a complete list of musicians and music-sellers which appeared in it :—

'Robert Bremner, music shop at the Cross.
John Clark, Organist, Blackfriars' Wynd.
Robert Hutton, Musician, Kennedy's Close.
Robert M'Intosh, Musician, Skinner's Close.
John M'Pherson, Musician, Bell's Wynd.
Neil Stewart, music shop, Parliament Close.
John Smiton (Smeaton),[1] Musician, Henderson's Land.
George Cooper, Music-master, back of the Exchange.
John Grewar, Musician, entry to Gavinloch's Land.'

These were the musicians known to be living in

---

[1] A descendant of the famous Principal Smeaton of Glasgow who died in 1583, and cousin of John Smeaton, the builder of Eddystone Lighthouse.

The Players and the Singers 107

Edinburgh in 1774 : not one is entered as a teacher of singing; the majority of them we may therefore conclude were instrumentalists who earned their daily bread by playing for it, and if so, we seem fully justified in believing that in the list before us we have the names of the very men who formed the nucleus of the orchestra in this old place twelve years after the hall was built.

Two things strike us as very interesting when we scan this list: first, that all these men lived within a few hundred yards of the Niddry Wynd; and in the second place, that the number of professional musicians in 1774 is surprisingly large, both absolutely, and especially relatively to the numbers of members of other professions in Edinburgh.

The large number in 1774 is still more striking when compared with the list of musicians in 1805, four or five years after the hall was closed.

It is as follows, from the Edinburgh Directory of 1805 :—

'G. Stabilini, 1 North St. James's Street.
Urbani and Liston, Music-sellers, 10 Princes Street.
N. Corri, Music-seller, Concert Rooms, Leith Walk.
William Clark, Music teacher, 6 James Street.'

No concert—no orchestra. Of these not one is entered as a 'musician'; Urbani, Liston, and Corri appear as music-sellers; Stabilini and William Clark we know were instrumentalists—they are but two.

This corresponds exactly with what we know about the dead state of music, and indeed of all art, at this time in Edinburgh: we cannot but feel the sharpness of the contrast with its very vital state thirty years earlier, when the St. Cecilia concerts were in full swing.

The century had opened gloomily: the political stability of Europe was being threatened by the insane ambition of one man, through whom this country was being drained of money, and thrown into a state of acute depression which affected all departments of life, but, naturally, more especially the departments of Art.

The Professional Vocalists.

By far the greatest of the professional singers who ever sang at St. Cecilia's was GIUSTO FERDINANDO TENDUCCI. He was born in the town of Sienna about 1736, and died early in this century somewhere in Italy. From the place of his birth, he was sometimes known in his own country as 'Senesino.' He had been trained in singing by Ferdinando Bertoni, a celebrated Italian singing-master. In 1758, Tenducci came over to London, where his magnificent voice almost at once won for him critical recognition. He supplanted a singer Guadagni, and became the hugely paid, fashionable idol of the hour. His first public

TENDUCCI,
*(From an Engraving in the British Museum after a Painting by
T. Beach of Bath, 1782.)*

The Players and the Singers 111

appearance was in a piece called *Attalio*, but it was not until he had sung in the opera *Ciro riconosciuto*, which was performed in the beginning of 1759, that his first-rate talents were fully perceived. In 1764 he met Mozart in London, and in 1784 and 1791 sang in the Handel Festivals. Previously he had 'made a hit,' singing in Dr. Arne's *Artaxerxes*, and shortly afterwards accompanied Arne upon a tour to Scotland and Ireland, which brought him back to London in 1765. He paid several visits to Edinburgh, staying occasionally, according to some accounts, with the noble family of Hopetoun, whom Thomson describes as his 'patrons,' and on these occasions always gave one or two concerts in the Niddry Wynd.

Thomson describes these as causing quite a 'sensation' amongst the local musicians, and continues:—
'I considered it a jubilee year whenever Tenducci arrived, as no singer I ever heard sang with more expressive simplicity, or was more efficient, whether he sang the classical songs of Metastasio, or those of Arne's *Artaxerxes*, or the simple melodies of Scotland. To the latter he gave such an intensity of interest by his impassioned manner and by his clear enunciation of the words, as equally surprised and delighted us. I never can forget the pathos and touching effect of his "Gilderoy," "Lochaber no more," "The Braes of Ballenden," "I'll never leave thee," "Roslin Castle."

These, with the "Verdi prati" of Handel, "Fair Aurora" from Arne's *Artaxerxes*, and Gluck's "Che faro," were above all praise.'

So high was Tenducci's art, his morals could not approach it: he was extravagant and dissipated, and in 1776 had to leave England in debt.[1] He returned, however, and published a *Treatise on Singing* and the *Ranleigh Songs*, which he had composed. In 1778 he again met Mozart, this time in Paris, when the great master composed a song for him that has been lost.

In the recently published *Life of Robert Fergusson* by the late Dr. Alexander Grosart,[2] there occurs a most interesting mention of this eminent singer:—'More suggestive still—as it was my privilege first to publish —Tenducci became his (*i.e.* Fergusson's) friend—that Tenducci who first directed the attention of George Thomson to the Scottish melodies, and so indirectly became the originator of his great work.' . . . 'It is to be here recorded that to the opera *Artaxerxes*, which was produced in 1769 with many attractions in the Theatre Royal, Edinburgh, Fergusson contributed three songs.' It appears to have been Fergusson's words to the airs 'Braes of Ballenden,' 'Roslin Castle,' and 'Lochaber no more,' that Tenducci sang. Grosart speaks of Tenducci's friendship for

[1] *Biographical Dictionary of Musicians* (Brown).
[2] Oliphant, Anderson, and Ferrier, 1898, p. 87.

The Players and the Singers

Fergusson as being an established thing in 1769, and says that long after Fergusson's death in 1774 the great singer could not speak of the ill-fated young poet without weeping. Grosart further mentions Madame Tenducci, and he says that she also sang in the production of *Artaxerxes* mentioned above.

The following is the title of the publication containing the songs of Fergusson :—

'*Artaxerxes*, an English Opera, as it is performed at the Theatre Royal, Edinburgh. The music composed by Tho. Aug. Arne, Mus. Doc., with the addition of three favourite Scots airs. The words by Mr. R. Fergusson. Edin. : printed by Martin & Wotherspoon. 1769. Duodecimo.'

The performers were :—*Artaxerxes*, Mr. Ross; *Artabanes*, Mr. Phillips; *Arbaces*, Mr. Tenducci; *Rimenes*, Mrs. Woodman; *Mandane*, —— ——; *Seniera*, Miss Brown.

The actress whose name is left blank was Madame Tenducci. The part of *Mandane* was written by Arne expressly for his celebrated pupil Miss Brent, who became Mrs. Thomas Pinto.

But Tenducci *resided* on several occasions in Edinburgh, and practised his profession as a teacher of singing. In *Kay's Portraits*[1] we have a very interesting side-light upon the genial Italian's life in this city. The subject of the sketch is 'Mr. John Campbell,' who

[1] Vol. ii. p. 92.

in 1775 became the precentor of the Canongate Parish Church, and of whom the writer says:—'John Campbell, . . . along with his brother Alexander, . . . became a pupil of the celebrated Tenducci, a fashionable teacher *who remained in Edinburgh* for some time. . . . The charge for each lesson was half a guinea, but the Italian exhibited a degree of considerate partiality for the musical brothers by affording them instructions at half-price.' Both the brothers Campbell were present, according to Stewart Watson's picture, on the evening of Burns's installation as poet-laureate to the Freemasons' Lodge, an occasion to which we have so frequently alluded.

Tenducci must have been possessed of that order of kind-heartedness which expresses itself in outward acts involving some considerable amount of personal trouble. He was anxious, before he left Edinburgh, to see his friend Campbell of the Canongate earning a larger income, and thereby justified in going the length of establishing a Mrs. Campbell. He accordingly induced the worthy precentor to sit to Allan the painter for his portrait, which Tenducci had engraved and below it had written, 'C—p—ll, P—n—r, C—g—e C—h.' This, as a 'Circular,' he despatched to most of the well-known people in town, the Duchess of Gordon, Lady Wallace, the Earl of Hopetoun, and Sir John Halket, among others. Tenducci left Edin-

The Players and the Singers 115

burgh without ever telling Campbell what he had done, the result being that the astonished precentor of the Canongate received a number of letters requesting his 'professional services.'

The writer adds in a footnote:—'Tenducci was an unrivalled singer of old Scottish songs, such as "Flowers of the Forest," "Waly, waly, gin love be bonny," "The Lass o' Patie's Mill," "The Braes o' Bellendean," "Water parted from the sea," "One day I heard Mary say," "An thou wert my ain thing."'

O'Keefe in his *Recollections* says:—'About the year 1766 I saw Tenducci in Dublin as "Arbaces" in *Artaxerxes*, which I had seen in London on its first coming out at Covent Garden in 1762. His singing "Water parted" was the great attraction, as were the airs he sang as the first spirit in *Comus*. At his benefits there he had thirty, forty, and fifty guineas for a single ticket. The frolicsome Dublin boys used to sing about the streets to the old tune of "Over the hills and far away":—

'"Tenducci was a piper's son
And he was in love when he was young,
And all the tunes that he could play
Was "Water parted from the *say*."

In 1784 I knew Tenducci in London, when he set to music Captain Jephson's *Campaign*.'

Seeing that Dr. Arne and Tenducci travelled

together in 1765 in Scotland and Ireland, we may assume it for a certainty that when in Edinburgh with the great vocalist, Dr. Arne would be present at a St. Cecilia concert, if not as conductor of some things from his own *Artaxerxes*, then surely as an honoured guest.

Tenducci turns up once more in quite another situation, for 'when Smollett was confined in the King's Bench Prison (1758-59) for libel upon Admiral Knowles,' says Chambers in the *Traditions*, 'he formed an intimacy with the celebrated Tenducci.' The vocalist had been imprisoned for debt, but Smollett took pity upon him to the very practical extent of paying his debts, and so procuring his release. Years afterwards Tenducci was singing in an Edinburgh drawing-room, and when some one told him that a lady present was a relative of his benefactor, the grateful Italian, at once advancing before her, seized her hands and covered them with kisses in a manner so wholly un-Scottish, that the good lady was not a little embarrassed in presence of a roomful of people ignorant of the cause of it all. It is extremely probable that during Smollett's visit to Edinburgh in 1766 he would attend a concert or two at St. Cecilia's, the place which his devoted *protégé* could, even alone, have made famous.

Stenhouse, writing in Johnson's *Scots Musical*

The Players and the Singers 117

Museum, quotes Charles Kirkpatrick Sharpe on Tenducci thus:[1]—

'Ferdinando Tenducci.—This was, as far as I know, the only very celebrated Italian singer who ever visited Scotland. His arrival is thus announced in the *Edinburgh Evening Courant*, Monday, May 16, 1758.[2] "Last night arrived here from Ireland, Mr. Tenducci, the celebrated singer."

'Along with him he brought his wife, whom he had married in Ireland: she also sang in public, but with a very indifferent voice, as I have been told by those who heard it. Her extraordinary platonic passion ended in an elopement with a gallant, and in a divorce which makes a figure in the trials for adultery, etc. Tenducci was a very handsome man; she a pretty, modest-looking girl. He taught music while in Edinburgh; and published a folio volume of his own compositions of which this is the title—" A collection of lessons for the Harpsichord or Piano and forte composed by Ferdinando Tenducci: Dedicated to the Right Honourable Lady Hope: Printed for the author, and to be got at his lodgings opposite Lord Milton's, Canongate; at Mrs. Phin's, and Richard Carmichael, engraver, back of the guard, and at R. Bremner's music shop." Minuets are mingled with sonatas, but only two have the names of

[1] Vol. iv. p. 107.
[2] A printer's error for '1768,' the correct date.

ladies prefixed—Ladies Hope and Cunningham (Miss Myrton of Gogar). Lady Cunningham's minuet with variations is extremely beautiful.—(C. K. S.)'

Between May 1768 and 1785, Tenducci was heard a good many times in Edinburgh both on the concert platform and on the operatic stage. His engagements are advertised in the *Edinburgh Evening Courant*, the first after his arrival bearing date May 21st, 1768:—
'(By particular desire of several persons of distinction) on Wednesday, the 25th May 1768, Mr. Tenducci will give a concert of vocal and instrumental music at St. Cecilia's Hall, Niddry's Wynd. Particulars of the entertainment will be expressed in the bills of the day. Tickets, price two shillings and sixpence, to be had at Balfour's coffee-house and at Mr. Tenducci's lodgings at Mrs. Reynold's in Miln's Square. To begin at six o'clock precisely.'

In the same paper on May 28th, 1768, the following appears:—'Mr. Tenducci set out this day for Ireland, but is engaged to return against the 28th of June when a concert is fixed for him,' after which the above-given details as to tickets, etc., are repeated.

The exact date in June of the great singer's return does not appear; but the issue of June 13th, 1768, contains the announcement of a concert in terms identical with the above, except that Tenducci's lodging is changed. 'Tickets may be had at Balfour's coffee-house and at Mr. Tenducci's house opposite to Lord Milton's lodgings, Canongate' (the famous Milton House).

On June 20 and 27 this announcement is repeated, with the additional information that 'Particulars of the entertainment will be expressed with handbills which will be given at the door the evening of the concert.'

The next announcement bears out what we know of Tenducci's practical kindness :—

'*July* 20*th*, 1768.—For the benefit of Mr. Olivieri (who is in a very bad state of health), on Wednesday next the 27th, will be performed a grand concert of vocal and instrumental music under the direction of Mr. Tenducci. . . . Mr. Tenducci acquaints that all the professors of music will not only perform on that night, but exert their utmost interest for a brother professor in distress who is not capable to wait on anybody.'

Tenducci at this time had 'come to stay'—a long time for him; for on August 6th, 1768, another announcement is made to the effect that 'Mr. Tenducci begs leave to inform the public that he intends to teach singing, and will attend ladies and gentlemen at their own houses,' his address being still in the Canongate opposite 'Lord Milton's lodgings.'

In the issue of the *Edinburgh Evening Courant* for December 5th, 1768, the following occurs :—'Mr. Tenducci's Concert is fixed for to-morrow se'nnight, being the 13th inst.'; and on December 21st we have: 'By order of the Governors and Directors of the Musical Society, Mr. Tenducci's second concert is fixed for Tuesday, 28th of February 1769.' Tickets were 2s. 6d.

Early in January of the next year we find Tenducci singing in a 'serious opera,' the *Royal Shepherd*, at the Canongate Theatre, and March 8th was a benefit night for him in this same piece. He had thus been fairly busy with concert and operatic singing in addition to his private teaching, but he had contrived to publish on April 17th, 1769, the work described above by C. K. Sharpe.

By June 7th, 1769, he is back to the locality which he first patronised, Mylne's Square, where tickets for a 'concert in St. Cecilia's Hall on Wednesday 21st, at which a new seranata will be performed, are to be got of Mr. Tenducci at his house in Miln's Square, first door up the scale stairs, back court.'

Mrs. Tenducci, 'who performs only on that occasion,' sustained one of the vocal parts, assisted by her husband, Miss Alphez, and Mr. Taylor.

About the middle of July 1769, Tenducci was unwell, and *Artaxerxes* was substituted at the theatre for some other opera in which he was to have sung. At the end of the month he had a benefit performance of *Artaxerxes*; and again on August 5th it was performed,

Tenducci taking the part of 'Arbaces.' The Tenduccis probably remained in Edinburgh until the following year, for on January 8th, 1770, 'Mrs. Tenducci's concert of vocal and instrumental music at St. Cecilia's Hall' on the 23rd of the month is advertised: address for tickets still Mylne's Square, back court.

In August 1779, Tenducci again appears in Edinburgh, lodging at Ann Street, New Town, but without his wife, and advertises that on 3rd September, by permission of the Governors and Directors of the Musical Society, there will be a benefit concert in St. Cecilia's for him and Signora Marchetti. On November 24th of this year Tenducci takes his benefit, and himself to Mrs. Stewart's, third door in Gavinloch's Land, Lawnmarket. In December 1779 he sings Scots songs at Mrs. Marchetti's concert, Mrs. Marchetti having Puppo to play a violin obligato to her singing. 'Tickets are to be had of Mrs. Marchetti at Mrs. Stewart's, Gavinloch's Land, Lawnmarket.' Oh! Mr. Tenducci, Mr. Tenducci, Oh!

In the *Caledonian Mercury* of August 6, 1785, Tenducci announces that on the 10th, at a benefit concert in St. Cecilia's Hall, he will present his patrons 'with a beautiful engraving by Mr. Bertalozzi, after a design of the celebrated Cipriani.' We infer that this is an engraving of Tenducci himself: the notice goes on politely to suggest that it should not be thrown away at the door. Tenducci was at this time living at 8 Princes Street.

There is an allusion to Tenducci in a very quaint appendix to Arnot's *History*, entitled 'A Dissertation on the Scottish Musick.' 'We sometimes find a foreign master who, with a genius for the pathetick and a knowledge of the subject and words, has afforded very high pleasure in a Scots song. Who could hear with insensibility or without being moved in the greatest degree, Tenducci sing "I'll never leave thee," or "The Braes of Ballendine"?'

ROBERT BREMNER, incidentally mentioned by Sharpe, was what we would nowadays call an 'agent' for musicians. Born in Scotland about 1720, he had been a pupil of Geminiani's and taught singing in Edinburgh, besides establishing himself in business as a musical publisher in premises opposite the head of Blackfriars' Wynd in the High Street.

He published, amongst other works, *Thoughts on the Performance of Concert Music*, inspired, no doubt, by his experience as agent for the Edinburgh Musical Society. About 1761 he went to London, but continued to make important engagements for the old Edinburgh Society, Schetky being one whom he sent down. He also published *The Rudiments of Music, with Psalmody* (1756); *A Collection of Scots Reels*; *A Collection of Scots Songs*.

Bremner died at Kensington Gore in May 1789.

'Miss Poole, Mr. Smeaton, Mr. Gilson, and Mr. Urbani were also,' wrote Thomson, 'for a time singers at the hall, chiefly of English and Scottish songs.'

The 'Mr. Urbani' of this sentence was a Signor PIETRO URBANI, who was born in Milan in 1749, and died in South Cumberland Street, Dublin, in 1816, according to one account 'in extreme poverty.'

The obituary of the *Scots Magazine* for 1816 thus notices his death :—' Died lately in South Cumberland Street, Dublin, aged 67, after a painful and tedious illness, which he bore with resignation, Peter Urbani, professor of music, a native of Milan in Italy, where he obtained the degree of Doctor of Music. The celebrated Rontzini and Urbani were the only remaining two of that great school of science. They finished their studies nearly about the same time, quitted their native home together, and arrived in London. After some years Rontzini went to Bath, Urbani to Edinburgh, where he resided for many years with distinguished *éclat*. He has left an aged widow behind, a foreigner, now deprived of everything, even the means of subsistence.'

Urbani seems to have come to Edinburgh about 1784 and to have resided there for some considerable time, probably until well on into the first decade of the present century, when he removed to Dublin. In 1785 Urbani was lodging in two different places, in April at Mrs.

Alexander's, First Turnpike, head of St. Mary's Wynd, and in July 'head of Warriston's Close, Luckenbooths,' but in 1796 his address is 'foot of Carrubber's Close.' In 1792 he was living in Carrubber's Close on the north side of the High Street. Urbani, besides singing as soloist at the St. Cecilia concerts, undoubtedly taught music and singing in Edinburgh, hence the designation 'Professor of Music'; and was moreover a well-known character in the convivial and artistic life of Edinburgh —two departments thereof that were never very far separated from each other.

Urbani seems to have been decidedly popular while in Edinburgh, and for several years prosperous, until he embarked on a very unsuccessful undertaking thus described in the *Lyric Poetry and Music of Scotland*:—
'In 1802 he and the late Mr. Sybold, the composer and harp-player, engaged a numerous and respectable band of vocal and instrumental performers from various parts of the kingdom, that the inhabitants of Edinburgh and Glasgow might be gratified with hearing some of the best oratorios of Handel, etc. This concern, though deserving of encouragement, did not succeed, and the affairs of both contractors were ruined. Sybold died that spring of a broken heart, and poor Urbani, after struggling with his misfortunes for some time in Edinburgh, was at length induced to settle in Ireland.'

The Players and the Singers 125

The old *Dictionary of Musicians* says of Urbani:—
'His taste in arranging Scotch music, and even in composing imitations of it, was highly considered at Edinburgh, where he published several volumes of Scotch melodies with new accompaniments, and some of his own airs intermixed. One of his most admired songs in the Scotch style is "The Red Rose," given in the *Vocal Anthology*.'

As a matter of fact, Urbani must have been very industrious during his time in Edinburgh, for he published between 1792 and 1804 six volumes of Scots songs, the full title of which is: 'A Selection of Scots Songs harmonised and improved with simple and adapted graces. Most respectfully dedicated to the Right Honourable (Elizabeth Dalrymple) the Countess of Balcarres, by Peter Urbani, professor of music. Book I. Entered at Stationers' Hall; Price twelve shillings.'

Book II. is dedicated to the Lady Catherine Douglas, daughter of the Earl of Selkirk.

Book III. is dedicated to the Hon. Lady Carnegie. Edinburgh, printed and sold by Urbani and Liston, 10 Princes Street.

Book IV. is dedicated to the Right Hon. Lady Lucy Ramsay.

Books V. and VI., published together as 'A select collection of original Scotch airs with verses, the most part of which were written by the celebrated Robert Burns,' were dedicated to the Duchess of Bedford.

Of Urbani's songs it has been remarked: 'Urbani's selection is remarkable in three respects—the novelty and kind of instruments used in the accompaniments; the filling up of the pianoforte harmony; and the use for the first time of introductory and concluding symphonies to the melodies.'

Urbani also published in Edinburgh 'A further selection of Scotch tunes, properly arranged as duettos for two German flutes or two violins, by P. Urbani. Book 1., Price 5s. . . . Printed and sold by Urbani and Liston' (Princes Street).

The notice to the old Scottish tune, 'Thou art gane awa'' (new set), in *Lyric Poetry and Music* runs thus:— 'This is the same air with the embellishments introduced by the late Mr. P. Urbani in singing the song at the concerts in Edinburgh. This gentleman published at Edinburgh in two folio volumes "A select collection of original Scottish airs for the voice, with introductory and concluding symphonies and accompaniments for the pianoforte, violin, and violoncello"—a work of great merit. In the preface he informs us that, having been struck with the elegant simplicity of the original Scots melodies, he applied himself for several years in attending to the manner of the best Scottish singers, and having attached himself to that which was generally allowed to be the best, he flattered himself that he had acquired the true national taste. He sung during a period of four years the Scots airs in the concerts of the Harmonical Society of Edinburgh, and for three years in the concerts in Glasgow. In both places he received such marks of universal applause as convinced him that his method of singing was approved by the best judges.'

Urbani is described as an excellent singer, and his knowledge of counterpoint is said to have been masterly and profound.

The tune, 'O can ye sew cushions?' was a great favourite of Urbani's, and he gave it a new accompaniment in his collection of songs.

Urbani, though unknown to Grove, was not unknown to Burns—indeed, Burns and he seem to have been very good friends. Urbani's name comes to be associated with the birth of two of the finest of Scottish songs, the one that magnificent ode, 'Bruce to his troops on the eve of the Battle of Bannockburn,' the other that sweetest and saddest of all songs, 'Ye banks and braes o' bonnie Doon.'

The circumstances attending the composition of the former are very well known, but they are so interesting that they warrant repetition *à propos* of our musician Urbani.

Burns and his friend Mr. Syme had been paying a

visit to the Earl of Selkirk at Mary's Isle in July 1793, and Mr. Syme thus writes of a musical evening at his lordship's :—' Urbani, the Italian, sung us many Scottish songs accompanied with instrumental music. The two young ladies of Selkirk sung also. We had the old song of "Lord Gregory," which I asked for, to have an opportunity of calling on Burns to recite his ballad to that tune ; he did recite it,' etc. etc.

On the 30th of July, Mr. Syme and our bard set out on horseback from the hospitable mansion of Mr. Gordon of Kenmore for Gatehouse, a village in the stewartry of Kirkcudbright. 'I took him,' says Mr. Syme, ' by the moor road, where savage and desolate regions extended wide around. The sky was sympathetic with the wretchedness of the soil, and it became lowering and dark. The hollow winds sighed, the lightnings gleamed, the thunder rolled. The poet enjoyed the awful scene. He spoke not a word, but seemed rapt in meditation. . . . What do you think he was about? He was charging the English Army along with Bruce at Bannockburn. He was engaged in the same manner on our ride home from St. Mary's Isle, and I did not disturb him. Next day (2nd August 1793) he produced me the following "Address of Bruce to his Troops," and gave me a copy for Dalzell.'

Burns, writing to Thomson the next month (Sept. 1793) and sending him a copy of the poem, says in allusion to the old Scottish air, 'Hey tutti taitie,' which he, in accordance with an old tradition, believed to have been Bruce's 'march' at Bannockburn, that, as played by Fraser on his hautboy, it often brought tears to his eyes.

In a postscript to the letter he says:—'I showed the air to Urbani, who was highly pleased with it, and begged me to make soft verses for it, but I had no idea of giving myself any trouble on the subject, till the accidental recollection of that glorious struggle for freedom, associated with the glowing ideas of some other struggles of the same nature, not quite so ancient,[1] roused my rhyming mania.'

We all know the rest of the story—how Thomson, disapproving of the tune Burns alluded to, desired him to lengthen the incisive final line of each verse to suit a tune 'Lewie Gordon,' which he thought more dignified. Burns in his great condescension actually complied with this fiat of bad judgment, and the mutilated version was published. After some years, however, Thomson was reconciled to the original tune in connection with which everybody knows the song.

Urbani is once again mentioned in a letter to Thomson (September 1793), in which also Burns makes direct allusion to the St. Cecilia's concert. . . .

[1] French Revolution.

'"Toddlin' hame": Urbani mentioned an idea of his which has long been mine, that this air is highly susceptible of pathos; accordingly you will soon hear him, *at your concert*, try it to a song of mine in the *Museum*, "Ye banks and braes o' bonnie Doon."' Here we are behind the scenes, as it were, in the manufacturing of a Scottish song. An old Scottish air is to be *tried* by an Italian musician for the first time in public at a forthcoming St. Cecilia's concert, to verses of Burns written years before. All the world knows that exquisite wedding of Scottish pathos in music to Scottish pathos in verse, 'Ye banks and braes,' but all the world does not know that it was first sung in 1793 by a now long-forgotten Italian, at one of the weekly concerts in the dreary old Niddry Wynd off the High Street of Edinburgh.

Urbani while in Dublin had two operas of his performed, *Il Fornace* and *Il Trionfo di Clelia*.

It will be noticed that Urbani's collection of Scottish songs clashed as to date with Thomson's, and accordingly we are not surprised to find that he and Thomson were by no means good friends. Thomson expresses himself as to Urbani as follows:—'. . . an Italian here who has published a water-gruel collection of these songs, and would see me at the devil on account of my collection' (1800).

Musicians, however, confess that Urbani's harmonising and accompaniments were very good indeed. Burns, no judge of singing beyond what every one feels about good or bad voice-production, thus writes of Urbani to Thomson (1793) :—'He is, *entre nous*, a narrow, conceited creature, but he sings so delightfully that whatever he introduces *to your concert* must have immediate celebrity.' In the same letter Burns admits that Urbani 'looks with rather an evil eye' on the collection: it was another case of 'two of a trade seldom agree.' The 'narrow, conceited creature' could on occasion be bold enough: he once sang a comic song!—*vide* the *Caledonian Mercury*, March 14th, 1785.

From Urbani we are led on to the name 'Corri.' Thomson's words are :—'Signor and Signora Domenico Corri from Rome; he with a falsetto voice which he managed with much skill and taste; the signora with a fine, full-toned, flexible soprano voice.' The family of Corri was a large one: various members of it appeared in, disappeared from, and reappeared in Edinburgh musical annals 'unto the third and fourth generation.'

DOMENICO CORRI was born at Rome on the 4th of October 1746, and died at Hampstead, London, in July 1825, as appears from the obituary of the *Scots Magazine* for that month :—'Suddenly, at Hampstead, Mr. D. Corri, well known as composer and teacher of eminence for the last fifty years in London and Edinburgh.'

The following facts are from an autobiography which he prefixed to *The Singer's Preceptor, or Corri's Treatise on Vocal Music*.[1] The son of a confectioner in a religious house, the Cardinal Portocaro nearly persuaded young Corri to study for the priesthood; but his musical aptitude early asserting itself, he found himself in Naples, a pupil of Porpora. In the house of this prince of singing-masters—himself a pupil of Scarlatti and the world-renowned master of Mingotti and Farinelli—Corri boarded for five years (1763-1767), and chiefly owed his introduction into the best English society at Rome to the fame of Porpora and the estimation in which that great singer was held by a section of our nobility.

Here Corri was patronised by the Duke of Leeds, the Duke of Dorset, and the celebrated Dr. Burney. Through these persons Corri was introduced to Prince Charles Edward and his brother Cardinal York. The Prince was at this time living in a strictly private fashion, and Corri spent many an evening with him, the prince playing the 'cello, Corri the harpsichord.

Following Corri's own narrative, we read:—'About this time (1780) the Musical Society at Edinburgh, wanting a singer and conductor for their concerts,

[1] In two vols., folio.

MDLLE. BACCHELLI.
(From a Miniature in the possession of Mr. Butti.)

The Players and the Singers 135

wrote to l'Abbé Grant at Rome, desiring him to obtain for them, if possible, either of the two persons mentioned by Dr. Burney. At the arrival of this letter, l'Abbé Grant found these two persons, namely Miss Bacchelli and myself, united in marriage. This circumstance being no impediment to the proposal from Edinburgh, . . . he immediately concluded for us an engagement for three years at Edinburgh, with a handsome provision for our journey. We accordingly left Italy about three months after, and arrived at Edinburgh, August 1781.'[1]

In Dr. Burney's *State of Music in Italy* there is a curious account of a ruse practised on Miss Bacchelli in order to allow a number of English gentlemen to hear her sing. Miss Bacchelli, a celebrated amateur singer, was so jealously guarded by her father that he would not allow any of the men to be introduced to her, so that even the learned and respectable Dr. Burney himself was for a time deprived of the pleasure of hearing La Bacchelli, or the Miniatrice, sing. The Duke of Dorset and Dr. Burney having got to know a favourite walk of Miss Bacchelli and her father, contrived on one occasion to have an orchestra ready in the neighbourhood, and actually managed to per-

---

[1] Mr. John Glen does not believe that Corri is here telling 'the truth, the whole truth, and nothing but the truth,' about himself and Miss Bacchelli.

suade the 'stern parent' to allow his daughter to sing. This she did, to the immense admiration of the Duke and the Doctor. Corri continues:—

'The second year of our Edinburgh engagement, proposals were made to me from London by Mr. Yates to compose for the Opera House, and by Messrs. Bach and Abel to Mrs. Corri to sing at the first opening of the Hanover Square Rooms. These proposals we were enabled to accept, through the kind indulgence of the Directors of the Edinburgh Society. After this season in London we again returned to Edinburgh, which engagement we continued for eighteen years.'

During that time Corri practically lived alternately in Edinburgh and London.

Dr. Burney writes[1] under date Rome, September 2nd, 1770:—'The day after my arrival at his Grace the Duke of Dorset's, I heard Signor Celestini (Celestino?), the principal violin here, who is a very neat and expressive performer. He was ably seconded by Signor Corri, who is an ingenious composer and sings in very good taste.'

Corri's memory as to the date of his arrival in Edinburgh is not to be trusted. He gives it as 1781: as a matter of fact, he performed or sang at almost every second concert given in Edinburgh during 1779.

As early as February 1779, 'Signor and Signora

[1] *State of Music in Italy.*

The Players and the Singers 137

Corri' sang at a benefit of Schetky's in St. Cecilia's Hall.

On March 25th, Corri had a benefit at the Theatre Royal, and his *Wives Revenged* had already been played.

On April 3rd, the *Edinburgh Evening Courant* announces a concert at the Theatre Royal, at which 'Mr. Corri will play a new-invented instrument by Dr. Walker, called the Celestino, being the only one in this country.'

In April 1779, Corri had a prolonged quarrel with a Mrs. Melmoth over the remuneration due her for singing at the theatre.

At two concerts at least, both in St. Cecilia's, Corri performed in July 1779; one of these was his benefit. At this time he was living at Abbeyhill.

It would be tedious to follow Corri's movements during the long time that he figures in Edinburgh musical circles; but taking the year 1785, we find 'Mr. and Mrs. Corri' as busy as ever. They sing at a concert of Clarke's on July 25th, 1785, and at a concert on March 15th of that year not only is 'Master Corri' announced to sing, but Signor N. Corri (Natali) plays in a trio—mandoline, guitar, and 'cello—by Signors Stabilini, N. Corri, and Schetky.

Corri's 'Ode,' as he called it, 'for four voices, of " Margaret and William,"' was given in St. Cecilia's on 10th February 1783, at a concert which was to have been Signora Corri's benefit, but postponed on account of that lady being 'indisposed.'

By this time the firm of Corri and Sutherland had been established. In 1790, Mr. Corri's address is given as 1 Rose Court; in 1799 it was 10 St. Andrew Square; but Mrs. Corri's and Natali's is 2 Shakespeare Square.

It appears that Corri was present in the musicians' group on the famous evening at St. John's Chapel, Canongate, and that his head was painted in Stewart Watson's picture of the scene. In the photogravure of the painting reproduced for MacKenzie's *History of the Lodge Canongate Kilwinning*, there is no face to be seen in the corner in which Corri should be, and where he is described as being in *A Winter with Burns*. Corri is not indicated in any key to the picture, but in our photographic reproduction from the engraving of the painting, his face, though not very distinct, can be made out. In *A Winter with Burns* the following is found in the letterpress (but not key) description of the figures in the painting :—

'Behind the Italian fiddler an extra head may be seen in the picture, raised to obtain a glimpse of the ceremony. This is Signor Corri, an Italian composer, teacher, and dealer in music. He built the rooms appropriated to musical, theatrical, and equestrian entertainments, which went by the name of Corri's

MUSICIANS' GROUP AT LEFT SIDE OF ORGAN GALLERY, FROM STEWART WATSON'S PICTURE.
1. James Tytler, Author, etc.
2. Signor Corri.
3. Thomas Neil, Precentor of Old Tolbooth Church.
4. Signor Stabilini, Violinist.
5. Allan Masterton, Composer.
6. John Dhu, Grand Tyler.

The Players and the Singers

Rooms, afterwards known as the Caledonian and as the Adelphi Theatre, Broughton Street. He took into partnership in the music business Mr. Henderson. Corri latterly became bankrupt. During the week of Burns's arrival in Edinburgh he was advertising the arrival of ladies' portable harpsichords, suitable for carrying in a post-chaise.'

Domenico or 'Old Corri' composed and published a good deal, although little of it nowadays is ever mentioned. His opera *Alessandro nell' Indie* did not, even in its own day, attract much attention when given in London in 1774; his musical extravaganza, *The Wives Revenged*, was produced in 1778 at the Theatre Royal, Edinburgh. He also composed an opera, *The Travellers*. In 1788 he published three volumes of English songs, and in 1797 entered into partnership with Dussek of the musical publishing-house, but Corri was at no time very successful financially. He wrote much for English, French, and Italian songs, which Dussek and he published.

His brother, who arrived in Edinburgh in 1790, was Natali Corri—'Young Corri' of Edinburgh records. Domenico's children included:—

> MONTAGUE CORRI, second son, born at Edinburgh, 1784, resided successively in Newcastle, Manchester, and Liverpool. He died in London, September 19th, 1849.

HAYDN CORRI, third son, born Edinburgh, 1785; died Dublin, February 1860.

ANTONIO CORRI (in America in 1824).

A DAUGHTER, born in Edinburgh in 1775, who became:
- (1) Mrs. J. F. Dussek; and
- (2) Mrs. John Aldis Moralt.

In Edinburgh annals the name Corri is best known in connection with rooms—'Corri's Rooms'—just as the husband of a very famous lady is known as Mrs. So-and-so's husband. These rooms stood at the head of Broughton Street, on the site of the present Theatre Royal. The history of *this* Theatre Royal, as well as that of the 'Old Theatre Royal,' opened at the end of the North Bridge, in Shakespeare Square (on the site of the present General Post Office), is told with a wealth of detail by J. C. Dibdin in his *Annals of the Edinburgh Stage*.

The history of Corri's Rooms may be said to begin with a building known as 'Stephen Kemble's Circus,' opened on January 21st, 1793, with Sheridan's *Rivals*. Natali Corri, about 1794, took over this so-called circus (for it was only a hall), and arranged in it a series of concerts and other entertainments—a venture that proved eminently unsuccessful. Although this was so, Natali Corri transformed the rooms structurally into a theatre, but with no better luck when performances came to be given in it. The fact is, Edinburgh was far too small and too poor a place to sustain at one and the same time the patronage of the old-established theatre in Shakespeare Square as well as Corri's Rooms, not to speak of a third seduction, card-parties and concerts, got up by Urbani in the Assembly Rooms in George Street.

Poor Corri, bitterly disappointed and laden with debt, seems to have been unfortunate in all he touched, and is reported to have once said, 'If I became a baker the people would give up using bread.' It would appear that this story about Natali Corri owes its publicity to the pen of no less a man than Sir Walter Scott. He is writing in 1828 on the subject of the success of his *opus magnum* :—'I trust it will answer, yet who can warrant the continuance of popularity? Old Nattali Corri, who entered into many projects and could never set the sails of a windmill to catch the *aura popularis*, used to say he believed that were he to turn baker, it would put bread out of fashion. I have had the better luck to dress my sails to every wind, and so blow on, good wind, and spin round whirligig.' After which J. G. Lockhart remarks : 'The *Corri* here alluded to was an unfortunate adventurer, who, among many other wild schemes, tried to set up an Italian opera at Edinburgh.'[1]

[1] J. G. Lockhart, *Life of Scott*, p. 688 (New Popular Edition, A. and C. Black).

In Corri's Edinburgh, public amusements were not considered necessaries of life as they are in ours; indeed, the theatre-goers of Edinburgh, until comparatively recent years, formed a very small fraction of the inhabitants, and were considered by the non-playgoing majority to be very frivolous and barely respectable people.

Corri's Rooms changed hands, but not name, when in 1809 Henry Siddons fitted them up at an expense of £4000 as a theatre, where performances were given at intervals for the next two seasons. This is the phase of it to which Sir Walter Scott alludes in a letter written from Ashestiel, August 15th, 1809, to Joanna Baillie:—'... The theatre will, I think, be quite a *bijou*. We supped in it as Corri's Rooms on the night of the memorable Oxonian Ball.'

In 1816 the Rooms were used for a *fête* given to the 78th Highlanders, or 'Ross-shire Buffs,' just returned from the campaign which Waterloo had so satisfactorily ended. The decorations were, for Edinburgh in 1816, on a very elaborate scale: hundreds of lamps, interspersed among festoons of the 42nd tartan, heraldic shields, and trophies of all kinds from the field of the 'king-making victory,' blazed down upon the youth, beauty, and fashion of Edinburgh. Scenery, too, was not wanting, for a landscape, which included a painting of Edinburgh Castle, occupied the stage. At eleven

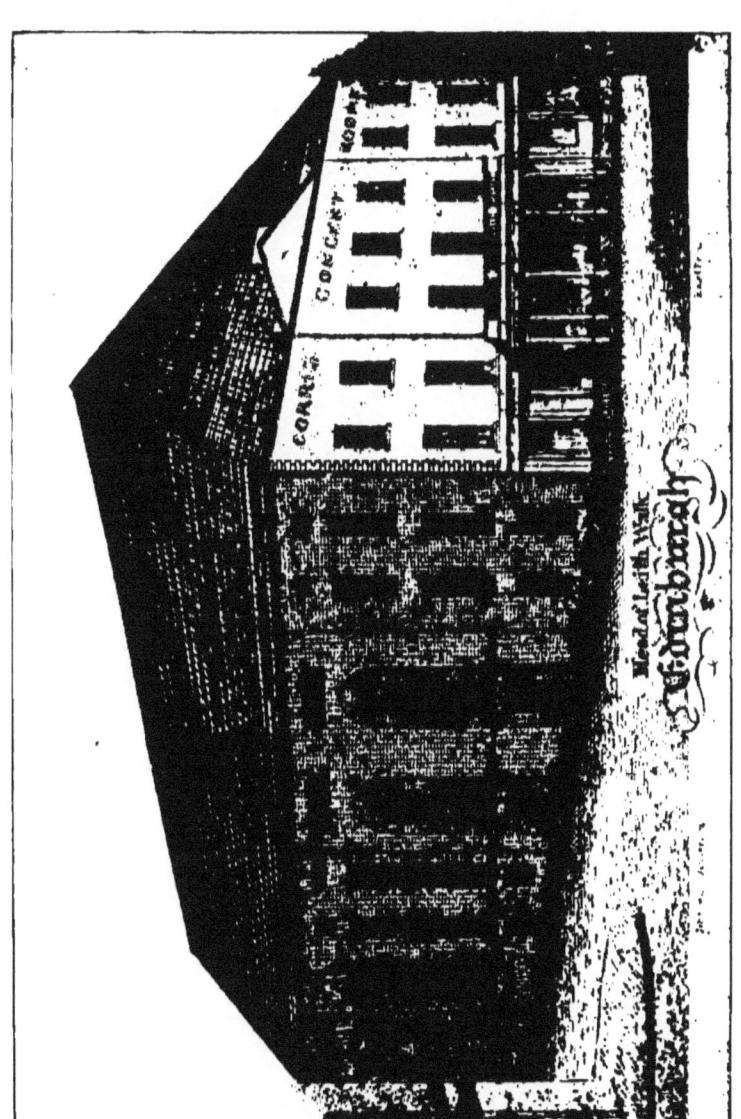

CORRI'S CONCERT-ROOMS, ON THE SITE OF THE PRESENT THEATRE ROYAL.
(*From an old piece of music.*)

o'clock in walked Neil Gow with his band of violins, and the ball began. The evening with the 78th in Corri's Rooms was long a milestone in the mental journey of many an Edinburgh belle.

At last the name was changed, and about 1820 Corri's Rooms became (in name only) the majestic 'Pantheon.' How it became the 'Caledonian Theatre' in 1823; then the 'Adelphi Theatre,' burned down in 1853; then the 'Queen's Theatre and Opera House,' burned down in 1865; then how it was rebuilt as the Theatre Royal, burned down in 1875, again rebuilt the following year, and, we fancy, once more burned down and rebuilt—it is not our purpose to relate in detail.

The name of Corri died hard in the Edinburgh annals: we keep on hearing of Patrick and Henry Corri, nephews of Natali, as well as of Kathleen Corri. Natali or Natale Corri died at Wiesbaden in 1822, aged fifty-seven, heavily in debt, and his elder daughter Frances (the younger was named Rosalie) would have been arrested, had not our good friend, old George Thomson, who had been security at the bank for her father, taken such steps as prevented this extreme measure being carried out. Thomson became in this way interested in the various changes and ultimate sale of the property known as 'Corri's Rooms.'

In Parke's *Musical Memoirs* [1] we have mention made

[1] Vol. ii. p. 5.

of Domenico Corri's *The Travellers, or Music's Fascination*, which was produced for the first time on 22nd January 1806, at Drury Lane Theatre.

This work professed to portray the kinds of music characteristic of the 'four quarters of the world.' At the time it was considered a very clever piece of composition.

In the same collection of musical anecdotes we find two allusions to 'Signora Corri':[1]—'1818. The Oratorios at Covent Garden Theatre began on Friday the 16th of February, with a grand selection in which Signora Corri, Miss Stephens, and Mr. Braham sang with effect.'

Again:—'The vocal concert . . . commenced at Hanover Square on the 6th March. The singers were Madame Fodor, Signora Corri . . .'[2]

With the names of MISS POOLE and CORNFORTH GILSON we may close our list of the professional singers and players of old St. Cecilia's. To the present generation this lady, either under her maiden name or her married one, Mrs. Dickons, is equally unknown, yet in her day she achieved considerable fame, as may be gathered from the tone of the notice of her in the old *Biographical Dictionary* already alluded to.

Besides possessing a fine voice, Miss Poole had

[1] Vol. ii. p. 13.   [2] *Ibid.* p. 132.

abnormally early developed musical powers, for at the age of six she could play Handel's overtures and fugues on the pianoforte. She was born in London in 1770, was a pupil of Ranzzini at Bath, and made her first public appearance in the *Messiah* on the 19th February 1790, in the 'Covent Garden Oratorios.'

Miss Poole made her operatic *début* in an opera of Shield's, *The Woodman*, at Covent Garden on 26th February 1791, where she appeared as 'Emily,' and was greatly praised both for her acting and singing. 'Religion seemed to breathe through every note,' said a contemporary with reference to her 'sublimity' in oratorio.

Miss Poole travelled in Scotland and in Ireland in the closing years of last century, apparently between 1794 and 1797, for in the latter year she was back in London singing in the *Messiah*. It was in the course of this tour that the English nightingale visited the Niddry Wynd.

In Dublin, in the Crow Street Theatre, she sang as 'Clara' in *The Duenna*, and was exceedingly well received. In 1816 she was engaged as *prima donna* at Madame Catalani's theatre in Paris; from that city she went on to Italy, where in Venice she received an ovation, and was by general vote proclaimed 'Socia Onoraria del Istituto Filarmonico.'

On October 12th, 1818, Mrs. Dickons made her

first appearance after her Continental tour, when she sang 'Rosina' in Rossini's *Barber of Seville*. Her style had matured, and she delighted every one. Parke the oboist, who knew her, includes her amongst the 'greatest singers England has produced, and whom I ever heard,' while he elsewhere says that he wrote a number of songs 'for that great singer Mrs. Dickons,' to be sung at Covent Garden, Drury Lane, at the Hanover Square concerts, and in the Dublin Theatre. She died in 1833.

The professional vocalist MR. GILSON seems to have resided in Edinburgh for a number of years, to have sung at many of the concerts, and to have taught singing in that city.

The date of Gilson's coming to Edinburgh is apparently fixed by the fact that about 1753 the Town Council passed an act 'for improving the church music in this city,' whereby the office of 'Master of Music' was created. The Musical Society were to examine candidates as to their fitness for the post, the result of their examination being that 'Cornforth Gilson from Durham' was elected.

Gilson, as early as 1759, published *Lessons on the Practice of Singing*, and in 1769 '*Twelve Songs for the Voice and Harpsichord*, composed by Cornforth Gilson, Edinburgh. Printed for and sold at Mr. Gilson's lodgings. Folio.' This is probably the only case on record of a book being 'printed for' a man's 'lodgings,' —Gilson's, in 1770, were in Skinner's Close.

Gilson gave many concerts, and participated in many more, both before and after the building of St. Cecilia's Hall. In the *Edinburgh Evening Courant* of December 17th, 1768, a concert of his own is announced in St. Cecilia's Hall on the 20th of the month, and on January 4th, 1769, he is announced to sing in a pretty elaborate concert in which Tenducci and Madame Doria were taking part.

The following musicians belong to the St. Cecilian epoch (1762 to 1800), and the list contains most of the names of such as have not elsewhere been dealt with. Those evidently foreigners are :—

Signor Arrigoni (opposite the British Linen Office, Canongate).

Signor Bianchi (*not* Francesco Bianchi who taught Sir Henry Bishop).

Signor and Signora Doria (in March 1765 in Chambers's Close ; in December in Tweeddale's Close; in March 1769, Morocco's Land, Canongate).

Signor Luciani (in 1770 at Mrs. M'Pherson's, Lawnmarket).

'Mrs.' Marchetti (in 1779 in Gavinloch's Land, Lawnmarket).

Mr. Martini Olivieri.

Signor Panelle (here in 1785 from Venice).
Signor Pescatore (in March 1765 in Skinner's Close).
Thomas Pinto.
Signor Torrigiani (in Edinburgh in February 1787,—
'his first appearance in this kingdom').
'Mr.' Tecklinburgh (in 1768 and 1770 at Mr. Aitken's, grocer, opposite Blackfriars' Wynd).
'Mr.' Scheniman.
Signor Sozzie (in Edinburgh in February 1790).
Signora Sultani (in Edinburgh in March 1787).
Mr. Vogel (a French emigrant who, in July 1796, gave a concert).

Of the rest, the following are presumably British :—
Mr. Aitken (long in Edinburgh; in 1765 in the Anchor Close, in 1796 in Gosford's Close, Lawnmarket; in 1796 he had a benefit concert in St. John's Chapel, Canongate).
Miss Alphez.
Miss Alsie.
Miss Barnet.
Miss Brent (later Mrs. Thomas Pinto).
Mrs. Collett.
Mr. Coobe.
Mr. Dow (in 1765 in Blackfriars' Wynd).
Mr. Fischer (Gavinloch's Close).
Mr. Frank (in 1769 in Niddry's Wynd).

The Players and the Singers 153

Mr. Fyfe (in 1765 in Clamshell Turnpike. He played on musical glasses).
Mr. Hutton (in 1768 in Old Assembly Close, in 1769 in Kennedy's Close).
Mr. Holland.
Mr. Meredith.
Mr. Muschet.
Mr. Rakeman ('master musician,' Royal Welsh Fusileers).
Mr. Sippe (master of band of 56th Regiment, in Edinburgh in 1787).
Mr. Sheener.
Mr. Smeaton (Smieton), (first fore-stair below head of Blackfriars' Wynd).
Mrs. Stuart (gave a concert in 1790).
Mr. and Mrs. Taylor.
Mr. Thomson (in 1770 Bailie Fyfe's Close, in 1796 Old Assembly Close).

The Amateur Players and Singers.

It appears that both in the orchestra and the chorus of the St. Cecilia concerts, Edinburgh amateurs took a very prominent part. The names of but few of these gentlemen have come down to us, but on Thomson's authority we can at least mention the Earl of Kelly, Gilbert Innes of Stow and 24 St. Andrew Square,

Alexander Wight, advocate, John Russell, W.S., John Hutton, paper-maker, and of course the redoubtable George Thomson himself.

As to George Thomson, he appears not only to have played the violin, but to have sung in the chorus. Innes, Wight, Russell, and Hutton also were prominent amateur members of the chorus.

As amateur musicians we shall be probably quite safe in including Hugh Dalrymple, Lord Drummore, and that Earl of Hopetoun who was the patron of Tenducci; but whether these noblemen ever played an instrument in St. Cecilia's Hall we have no evidence. Lord Drummore seems to have been held in high esteem by the 'Musical Society' of which he was the Governor, for on his death in 1755, 'the Society,' says Grant, 'performed a grand concert in honour of his memory, when the numerous company were all dressed in the deepest mourning.' The announcement for this is in the *Caledonian Mercury* of June 24th, 1755 :— 'The Directors of the Musical Society have appointed a Funeral Concert in Mary's Chapel on Friday the 27th instant, on the death of the Honourable Lord Drummore, their Governor. No member can have more than two ladies' Tickets. *N.B.*—The general meeting of the Society is adjourned till Wednesday the 2nd of July at 3 P.M.' We make further reference to this 'Funeral Concert' at page 206.

THOMAS ALEXANDER ERSKINE, SIXTH EARL OF KELLY.
(*From an Engraving by R. Blyth, after Home.*)

The Players and the Singers 157

THOMAS ALEXANDER ERSKINE, sixth Earl of Kelly, was born 1st September 1732, and died at Brussels 9th October 1781, in the fifty-first year of his age. Lord Kelly was an enthusiastic musician, of whom Dr. Burney wrote that he was possessed of more musical science than any man he had ever known. His mother was Janet Pitcairn, a daughter of the well-known wit, poet, and physician, Dr. Archibald Pitcairn, and from her he probably inherited his artistic bias. His musical taste was early developed, so that, as soon as he could, he went over to Manheim to study composition and violin-playing under the elder Stamitz, which he did to so much purpose that on his return to Scotland he was accounted the most proficient theoretical musician and instrumentalist of his time. He composed with astonishing rapidity, and preferably for wind instruments, but was quite careless about collecting and publishing his works, amongst which are an overture, the 'Maid of the Mill' (1761), and symphonies which were produced at Ranelagh and Vauxhall. His lordship is also credited with having composed songs, but in all probability much that he wrote is lost. He is known to have composed six overtures, and to have conducted one of them upon a certain occasion in St. Cecilia's Hall: symphonies, too, were amongst his productions.

The eccentric antiquary, Charles Kirkpatrick Sharpe

of Hoddam, did something to keep Lord Kelly's memory green, for he edited '*Minuets and Songs* now for the first time published with an introductory note by C. K. Sharpe, Edinburgh, 1839.' Nevertheless, there exists a work published in 1774 or 1775 entitled, '*The Favourite Minuets* performed at the Fête-Champêtre given by Lord Stanley at the Oaks, and composed by the Right Honourable the Earl of Kelly. Price two shillings. London: printed and sold by William Napier, the corner of Lancaster Court, Strand.'

Robert Bremner, in 1761, took out a royal licence for the sole publishing of Lord Kelly's compositions: from Bremner's press was issued a collection of *Six Overtures* by Lord Kelly.

Vigour, loudness, and rapidity characterise Lord Kelly's style. Some authorities think that his lordship wrote the words of the song, 'Kelso Races.'

Lord Kelly succeeded in 1756, and was never married.

It was after the death of Lord Kelly that the Musical Society performed one of their famous 'Funeral Concerts,' 21st December 1781—of course held in St. Cecilia's Hall.

Mr. Robert A. Marr, C.A., in *The Rise of Choral Societies in Scotland*,[1] has recorded some earlier

---

[1] *Music for the People*, p. 13 (John Menzies and Co., Edinburgh and Glasgow).

The Players and the Singers

'Funeral Concerts' given in the same place—one on 19th December 1766 for the well-known Lord Provost of Edinburgh, Sir George Drummond, who was also Depute-Governor of the Musical Society; and one on 22nd November 1771 for Sir Robert Murray, Bart., a director, and for William Douglas, the treasurer.

CHAPTER V

THE MUSIC PERFORMED AND SUNG IN ST. CECILIA'S HALL

THE names of most of the composers whose instrumental works were performed either in St. Mary's Chapel or St. Cecilia's Hall, either by the orchestra or by soloists, may be comprised in the following list:—

Corelli,	(1653-1713)
G. B. Bassani,	(1657-1716)
Geminiani,	(1680-1762)
J. S. Bach,	(1685-1750)
Handel,	(1685-1759)
Metastasio,	(1698-1782)
Arne,	(1710-1778)
Stamitz (the elder),	(1719-1761)
Stamitz (the younger),	(1746-1801)
Abel,	(1725-1787)
The sixth Earl of Kellie,	(1732-1781)
Haydn,	(1732-1809)
Vanhall,	(1739-1813)

The Music Performed and Sung 161

Mozart,	(1756-1791)
Pleyel,	(1757-1831)
Beethoven,	(1770-1827)

A very rich list, for it includes representatives of the older music, as also names yet heard in all series of classical concerts.

Of these composers, all except Corelli, Geminiani, Bach, Handel, and the elder Stamitz were alive when St. Cecilia's Hall was built.

The following are the names of composers whose *vocal* works were given by the Musical Society :—

Geminiani,	(1680-1762)
Handel,	(1685-1759)
Arne,	(1710-1778)
Gluck,	(1714-1787)
Paisiello,	(1741-1816)
Guglielmi,	(1727-1804)
Sarti,	(1729-1802)
Giornovicki (Jornelli),	(1745-1804)

Of these musicians all save the first two were living at the time the hall was built.

We are fortunate in being able to give a reduced facsimile page from a manuscript index of the music belonging to the Edinburgh Musical Society in 1782. The index, which is in the possession of Mr. Robert A. Marr, is in its original binding with rough calf back and corners, and consists of 128 pages post folio size. On the front board is a paper label, neatly printed by hand,

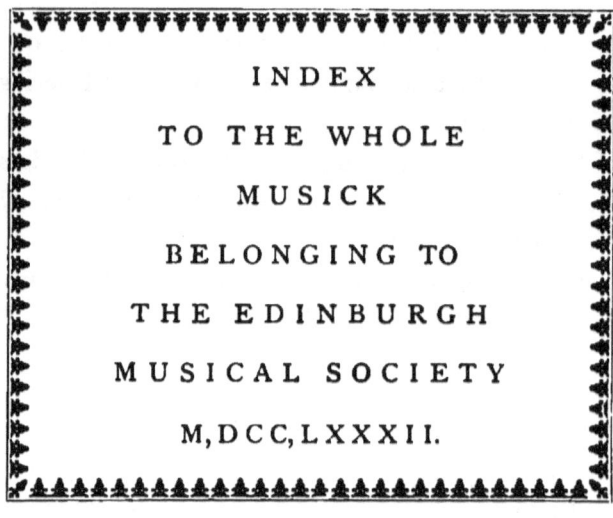

and inside the board the contents are given as follows :—

CONTENTS

1. Index of the whole music in alphabetical order.
2. Index of all the overtures.
3. Contents of all the music in score.
    N.B. The Quintetti and Quartetti in the letter Q : first Index. The Harpsichord Music : the leaf before the last Index.

The page reproduced is the index of all the overtures under the letter A, and a glance will show

Alphabetical List (overtures)	Authors Names	Numbers				
Abels 6 overtures op 1st		20	21	22	23	26
Do — 6 Do — op 4th		—	—	—	—	
Acis & Galatea	Handel	5	6	7	8	
Admetus — 1st		—	—	—	—	
Admetus — 2d		—	—	—	—	
Atius		—	—	—	—	
Alcina		—	—	—	—	
Alesandro	Cocchi & Bach &c.	20	21			26
Alexander	Handel	5	6	7	8	
——— Balus		—	—	—	—	
——— Feast		—	—	—	—	
——— Severus		—	—	—	—	
Almahide	do	34				
Amadis 1st	Handel	5	6	7	8	
——— 2d	do	26	34			
Ariadne		5	6	7	8	26
——— con Cornie Trombe	Porpora	34				
Arianna	Cocchi & Galuppi	20	21			26
——— Hasse Vinci &c.	Porpora	20				39
Ariodante	Handel	5	6	7	8	
Arminius		5	6	7	8	
Arnes 8 overtures		20				39
Artaserse	Bach	20	21			26
Artaxerxes	Arne	44	45	46		44
	Hasse vinci	34				
Astarto	Bach	20	21			26
	Bononcini	34	42			
Attilio (overt by)		34	42			
——— Regolo	Cocchi & Smell	20	21			26
Abels — 6 overtures op 7th		22	23	54	55	
——— 6 overtures op 10th	Abel	54	55			
——— 6 overtures op 14th		56				
Abels 6 Trios — op 8	Abel	49				

The Music Performed and Sung

how representative a collection the Musical Society possessed. The index has been most carefully compiled, and pencil jottings indicate that it has been in use until 1802. This was two years after the Society was dissolved, so that apparently one of its late members was in possession both of the pieces of music and of their index.

Certain of the composers' names before mentioned are household words, concerning which every one pretending to the 'pitifulest fraction' of culture knows something. Other names, however, we feel certain, call up few attendant facts in the minds of any persons who are not professedly musical specialists, and therefore a note or two upon some of these less-known musicians may be acceptable.

ARCHANGELO CORELLI was born in 1653 in the Italian city of Fusignano near Imola, and died on January 18th, 1713, in Rome, being buried beneath a monument in the Church of Santa Maria della Rotunda in that city.

Having studied music under Matteo, Simonelli, and Bassani, he travelled in Germany, but soon settled in Rome, where the greater part of his life was spent teaching music, like almost all his brethren of the fiddle-stick. One of his pupils—the greatest—was Geminiani. In Rome, Handel met Corelli and quarrelled with him, a thing quite in Handel's usual manner: the great German, like most geniuses, preferred his own way.

Corelli published his first series of sonatas in 1683, a second in 1685, a third in 1690, a fourth in 1694, and a collection of concertos, his last work, in 1712. He also left a number of gavottes.

Musical experts have a considerable meed of praise to offer to Corelli: he is described as a great violinist who laid down principles for the development of a much more elaborate technique, albeit in a purer style, than had previously been considered possible by the most ambitious executants. Corelli, in other words, created a new epoch in violin-playing by evolving potentialities in that instrument hitherto totally unsuspected, so that he is justly regarded as the founder of modern violin-playing and violin-composition.

Corelli is further reckoned as one of the greatest composers for the *solo* violin, notwithstanding that his chamber sonatas and his *concerti grossi* are by musical critics considered of high merit.

Musicians describe his style as possessing a 'quiet elegance,' pathetic in slow time, but confessedly dry in quick. During the whole of last century this composer was greatly in vogue—a popularity due in large measure to the zeal of his pupil and editor, Geminiani.

GIOVANNI BATTISTA BASSANI was born at Padua in 1657, and died at Ferrara in 1716.

CORELLI.
(*From an Engraving by Rothwell, from an original Painting.*)

The Music Performed and Sung 169

Thomson says it was his *motetti* that were played in the St. Mary's Chapel concerts.

He wrote much more than motets—cantatas and operas, besides a great deal for solo voice.

He was *maestro da capella* at Bologna Cathedral and subsequently at Ferrara. In 1682 he was appointed Director of the Academia dei Filarmonici at Bologna.

Bassani's music is described as religious in tone, 'with extreme delicacy in the management of pathetic effects.'

FRANCESCO GEMINIANI was born at Lucca in 1680, and died at Dublin in 1761. Geminiani had drunk to the full of the spirit of his famous master; but, though entirely 'of the school of Corelli,' he added to the characteristics of the Corellian manner of execution an unbounded vivacity of temperament. Tartini called him 'il furibundo Geminiani.' He was himself a very skilful violinist, and on coming to England in 1714 showed British musicians for the first time how Corelli ought really to be played, for, previously to this, that composer had been considered 'insurmountably difficult.'

Geminiani at the outset emphasised the rules Corelli had laid down for the actual handling of the violin, and he recommended holding the instrument on the left of the tail-piece. After having been for some little time in England, he was brought under the notice of Lord Essex, through whose influence he was appointed to the conductorship of the vice-regal band in Dublin Castle. He was not allowed to take up this post—probably because he was a Roman Catholic —and his pupil Dubourg got it instead. Geminiani had the honesty and gratitude to speak of Great Britain as his 'second Fatherland.'

Like so many of his order, Geminiani was most improvident. His hobby was buying pictures, and this would have brought him to the very verge of poverty had not Sir Robert Walpole come to his aid. Cecilia Young (Mrs. Thomas A. Arne) was a pupil of Geminiani.

His compositions include sonatas for violin, solos, and concertos; while his published works are:—*Il Dizionario, Rules for Playing in a true Taste,* and the *Art of Playing on the Violin,* the *Art of Playing on the Guitar,* and the *Art of Accompaniment,* which was translated into Italian, German, French, and Dutch.

Along with Geminiani in 1714, there came to England a performer on the tenor violin, FRANCESCO BARSANTI, who penetrated as far north as Edinburgh, where in 1742 he published '*A Collection of Old Scots Tunes,* with the bass for Violoncello or Harpsichord, set and most humbly dedicated to the Right Honourable the Lady Erskine by Francis Barsanti, Edinburgh.

METASTASIO.

The Music Performed and Sung 173

Printed by Alexander Baillie, and sold by Messrs. Hamilton and Kincaid. Price 2s. 6d. Folio.' Barsanti, also a native of Lucca, was born about 1690. By 1750 he had returned to London, so that he played not in St. Cecilia's Hall, but in St. Mary's Chapel.

The next composer we shall notice whose works were heard in the old hall is PIETRO ANTONIO DOMENICO BONAVENTURA METASTASIO, who was born in Rome in 1698, and died at Vienna 1782. It is as a dramatic poet and not as a composer that his name is most widely known; nevertheless, his genius had considerable range, for he sang, played on the harpsichord, and composed musical pieces. Born poor, he was educated by Vincenzo Gravina, the distinguished writer on Italian law. While still a lad, having written some poetry which attracted notice, he associated himself with the actress Madame Bulgarini, and devoted his attention to melodrama.

His dramas *Didone* at Naples, *Sirce* at Venice, *Catone*, *Semiramide*, and *Artaserse* at Rome (1730), were enthusiastically received. In 1729 the Emperor Charles VI. called him to Vienna, bestowed upon him the title of 'Cæsarean Poet,' with a liberal allowance. He thereafter settled at the imperial court, where, a great favourite, he was much honoured by the Empress Maria Theresa.

THOMAS AUGUSTINE ARNE, who was born in King

Street, Covent Garden, 1710, and died in London, 5th March 1778, was intended by his father for the profession of law. Young Arne, however, secretly taught himself to play the violin, and, on his father discovering this, was allowed to pursue the study of music, and was placed under the best masters. Arne's first production was the opera *Rosamond*, words by Joseph Addison, produced in Lincoln's Inn Fields Theatre in 1733, in which a younger brother and his sister Susanna Maria took parts. This lady was afterwards wife of Theophilus Cibber, son of Colley Cibber, the dramatist and poet-laureate. It was by her brother Thomas's advice that she studied tragedy, in which her father-in-law, actor as well as writer, gave her lessons.

Arne's next production was the *Opera of Operas*, but his music to *Comus* (1738) first showed his talent. Its success was immediate, and its popularity long-sustained. In 1759 the University of Oxford conferred upon him the degree of Doctor of Music. In 1762 Dr. Arne composed the opera of *Artaxerxes*—the first in the Italian style by an Englishman for English people, and in this our old St. Cecilia hero, Tenducci, sang. The very popular *Love in a Village* followed *Artaxerxes*.

Dr. Arne is indissolubly associated with English music. He practically initiated an era in operatic composition, and his having written 'incidental music'

DR. ARNE.

(From an Engraving in the possession of Captain Spencer V. F. Henslowe.)

The Music Performed and Sung

to five plays of Shakespeare will ever retain his name in the best literary company.

He wrote the music to the songs in *As You Like It* in 1740; to those in the *Twelfth Night* in 1741; in the *Merchant of Venice*, 1742; in the *Tempest*, 1746; in *Romeo and Juliet*, 1750. Everybody knows Dr. Arne's 'Where the bee sucks, there lurk I,' from the *Tempest* (Ariel's song); also 'Blow, blow, thou Winter Wind,' and 'It was a lover and his lass,' from *As You Like It*, and the clown's 'Come away, come away, Death,' from the *Twelfth Night*.

Still more widely known is the air, 'Rule Britannia,' which Arne composed for the song by James Thomson in a play, *The Masque of Alfred*, the joint production of Thomson and Malloch (Mallet), first performed August 14th, 1740, before Frederick, Prince of Wales. Arne composed this music at the Prince's residence, Cliveden House.

Dr. Arne, it is said, rearranged an old air into that of 'God Save the Queen' (King); but there is, I find, no little evidence to prove that the original words and music of the 'National Anthem' were by Anthony Young, Dr. Arne's wife's grandfather, who was organist of St. Clement's Dane and St. Catherine Cree near the Tower, London.[1]

---

[1] Cf. *The National Ode and the National Hymn, and who composed them*, by the Rev. W. H. Henslowe, M.A., vicar of

Arne wrote two oratorios, *The Death of Abel* and *Judith*, very little heard of nowadays. In 1740 he married Cecilia Young, daughter of Charles Young, the organist of All Hallows', Barking, London. Young had been frequently employed by Handel to play the organ parts in his oratorios. Cecilia was one of the singers in Arne's *Comus*.

After a visit to Ireland, Dr. and Mrs. Arne returned to London in 1744, and entered into an engagement at Drury Lane, and afterwards at Vauxhall, 'as musical composers.'

During this time Arne wrote much—ballads, cantatas, duets, and trios, publishing them in an annual collection called *Lyric Harmony*. Dr. Arne lies buried in St. Paul's Church, Covent Garden.

There were two musicians of the name of Stamitz, father and son.

JOHANN STAMITZ was born in 1719 in Deutschbrod, a small town in Bohemia, where his father was a schoolmaster. By 1756 he had established himself at Manheim as chamber-musician and conductor of the concerts, and was recognised as the founder of the violin school at Manheim, which a hundred and

Wermigey, Tottenhill, King's Lynn, Norfolk. The claim of Henry Carey to the authorship of this famous 'air' has been by many accepted as settled, but the point cannot yet be said to be decided. The earliest claimant is Dr. John Bull, organist to the Chapel-Royal (1591).

fifty years ago enjoyed quite a high reputation. Its fame attracted the Earl of Kelly as a young man from far Edinburgh, and he studied music under Stamitz himself.

This 'professor' of music published symphonies, overtures, concertos, quartets, and trios which are described by the old *Dictionary* as having 'deservedly attained celebrity,' but 'though truly masterly,' it continues, 'they are still of the old school, and are considered by some critics to savour too much of the church style.' It is Johann's compositions that Thomson alludes to as having been played in old St. Cecilia's before the arrival of Haydn's or the more modern music. This musician was considered quite a successful orchestral composer. He died at Manheim in 1761. Speaking of François Cramer, the old *Biographical Dictionary* says, 'He made himself well acquainted with the . . . capriccios of Benda and old Stamitz.'

CARL STAMITZ, elder son of the preceding, was born at Manheim in 1746, and studied the violin under his father.

In 1770 he went to Paris, and there for many years sustained a reputation as an instrumental composer as well as 'concerto player on the violoncello and tenor.' Some of his works were published at Paris, some at Berlin, some at Amsterdam.

There is little doubt it was this Stamitz the younger who was in London about 1784, for in Parke's *Memoirs* we are told that in that year in London instrumental music had 'arrived at a high degree of perfection,' chiefly through the talents of certain solo players therein enumerated. The list closes with 'Stamstz and Shield on the tenor.' This was one of Carl's instruments, and, mentioned in connection with so rare a name—though apparently misspelt,—leaves us in no doubt that it is Stamitz the younger who is alluded to. He died in South Germany, in Jena, while on a journey to Russia in 1801. His compositions are described as having fire and spirit, and as being more in keeping with modern feeling than those of his father —a very natural thing.

KARL FRIEDRICH ABEL, who was born at Kothen in Anhalt in 1725, and who died in London about 1787, was another of the foreign composers of lesser note whose pieces this old hall has heard. He was a famous player on the viol-da-gamba, and in the threequarter-length portrait of him by Gainsborough is represented playing upon this instrument. In conjunction with Johann Christian Bach he gave a series of successful concerts in London (1762-1782), in which Bach played the harpsichord and Abel the viol-da-gamba. His first public performance was in Dresden, whence in 1761 he came over to England, where the Duke of York procured him the post of 'Director of the Queen's Band.' Grove states he was appointed 'chamber-musician to Queen Charlotte' (wife of George III.) in 1765. J. B. Cramer was a pupil of Abel.

Abel had, it would appear, an enormously exaggerated opinion of his own talents, for on one occasion, having been challenged to perform something, he replied: 'Vat, shallenge Abel! dere ish but one Gott and one *Abel*.'

JOHANN BAPTIST VANHALL (Wanhal) was born at Nechanicz in Bohemia in 1739, and died at Vienna in 1813. Though he is said to have been of Dutch extraction, most of his life was spent in Vienna, where he composed a goodly number of works, which in England enjoyed considerable popularity immediately preceding the introduction of Haydn's music. It was in England indeed that much of Vanhall's work was published—symphonies, quartets, trios, duets, solos, and sets of sonatas for the harpsichord. Although his name is hardly ever mentioned nowadays, Vanhall was considered by contemporaries to have combined pleasing harmony and considerable melody in a 'free, manly style,' for he was a violinist as well as a composer. The old *Biographical Dictionary* speaks of the 'spirited, natural, and unaffected symphonies of this excellent composer.' He is accredited with quite a number of operas—nine or more—and a hundred symphonies, besides quartets and masses.

IGNACE or IGNAZ JOSEPH PLEYEL, born 1757, died 1831, was another composer whose music was heard at St. Cecilia's. At an early age he evinced musical ability, and studied music in Vienna under Vanhall and Haydn. After residence in Italy, he was made *Kapellmeister* at Strassburg, where he wrote a large number of compositions for the harpsichord. In 1791 he came to London to conduct the 'Professional Concerts' of the season, and on the first occasion did so in the presence of Haydn, upon 13th February 1792.

Mozart thought so much of Pleyel, that he declared he would do 'to succeed Haydn,' and certainly he copied that master so closely as to preclude originality. Considering himself ill-treated in Strassburg, he removed to Paris, where he founded the firm of pianoforte makers, 'Pleyel and Co.' His eldest son was Camille (born 1788, died 1855); and Camille's wife (born 1811) became a great pianist, and died only in 1875.

Pleyel, as we have said, wrote a number of airs for the Thomson collection of Scottish songs, and in this connection is twice mentioned in letters of Burns. In letter viii. (April 1795) Burns writes:—'One hint let me give you—whatever Mr. Peyel[1] does, let him not

---

[1] Mistake for Pleyel?

I. J. PLEYEL.

(*From an Engraving in the British Museum by W. Nu the Painting by T. Hardy.*)

alter one *iota* of the original Scottish airs.' Again, in letter xvi. (May 1794) he writes:—'I am quite vexed at Pleyel's being cooped up in France, as it will put an entire stop to our work.' A writer in 1793 speaks of 'the popular writers on the Continent, Haydn, Pleyel,' etc.

PIETRO GUGLIELMI, son of Joachim Guglielmi (musician to the Duke of Modena), was born at Massa di Carrara in 1727, and died at Rome in 1804. Having studied music with his father until he was eighteen, he was sent to the famous conservatoire of Loretto at Naples, the same which trained his contemporaries, Cimarosa and Paisiello. Here he was drilled in counterpoint and composition, but not until ten years later did he evince any power for original musical work. On quitting the conservatoire, however, he began at once to compose for the principal theatres of Italy. His operas, both serious and comic, were equally successful, and most of them were produced during the period of his rivalry with Paisiello, who seemed to regard the patronage of the theatre of Naples as his own special monopoly. No sooner did Paisiello compose an opera, than Guglielmi had one to dispute its claims to popular favour.

Guglielmi's fame spread considerably, for he was invited to Vienna, to Madrid, and to London, returning to Naples from a prolonged tour when in his fiftieth year. In the opinion of many, some of his operatic works were finer than the corresponding ones of Paisiello.

In 1793, Pope Pius VI. offered him the post of *maestro di capella* at St. Peter's, which he accepted. This gave him the opportunity of composing more especially for the church, and in the comparative leisure of this congenial post he spent the last eleven years of his life.

Guglielmi's collected works exceed two hundred. Two oratorios of his should be mentioned, *The Death of Holofernes* and *Deborah*, the latter being regarded by some as his *chef-d'œuvre*. Parke the oboist tells us that in 1813 'the King's Theatre opened on the 6th of January with Guglielmi's serious opera *Sidagero*.' Experts describe Guglielmi's music as having a clear and supported harmony, simple and elegant melodies, while originality characterises not a few pieces.

GIOVANNI PAISIELLO, one of the most famous musicians of the Neapolitan school, was born at Tarento in 1741, and died at Naples in 1816. Heredity cannot account for his great gifts in composition, for he was the son of a veterinary surgeon in the service of Charles III. of Naples. His father sent him to the Jesuit College at Tarento, where it was discovered that he had a fine contralto voice. In June 1754 he was placed under

Durante in the conservatorio of St. Onofrio; before 1763 he had composed masses, psalms, oratorios, motets, and 'a comic interlude,' and in that year he composed his first opera, a piece for the theatre at Bologna. Then for the theatres at Venice, Naples, Rome, Milan, Bologna, Modena, Parma, an immense number of operas were all written by the middle of 1776.

In July of that year he accepted service as musician in the court of Catherine II. at St. Petersburg, with an income from one source and another of nine thousand roubles.

Amongst the operas of the pre-Russian epoch may be mentioned *La Pupilla*, *Il Marchese Tulpiano*, and *La Semiramide*. Paisiello had actually been engaged to compose for the King's Theatre, London, but his invitation to the Russian imperial court caused him to forego the English engagement. During his stay in Russia, Paisiello composed several operas and a good deal of music for the harpsichord. *Il Barbiere di Siviglia*, an opera, and *La Passione*, an oratorio to Metastasio's words, both belong to this period.

After a sojourn in Vienna, where he wrote an opera for the Emperor Joseph II., he returned to Naples, and was immediately taken into the service of King Ferdinand IV. as *maestro di capella*. Hardly had this post been secured when an invitation arrived from

King William of Prussia begging him to come to Berlin. This he had to refuse, as also an invitation to go to Russia for the second time.

He remained in Naples until 1789, when King Ferdinand was deposed and a republican form of government established, the members of which requested Paisiello to regard himself as 'composer to the nation.' To this he agreed; but on the restoration of the Bourbons he found himself punished for what was considered disloyalty, and in consequence deprived of his appointments.

Napoleon, as First Consul, invited him to Paris, where we next find him composing a 'Te Deum' and a 'Grand Mass' for two choirs. He continued to live in Paris until after Bonaparte was declared Emperor, for whose coronation ceremony he composed some music.

Joseph Napoleon, as King of Naples, confirmed to him his appointments of *maestro di capella*, composer of the music of the chamber, at a salary of 1800 ducats. Napoleon sent him the Legion of Honour, and honours poured upon him from home and foreign musical societies. On 30th December 1809 he was elected Associate of the Institute of France.

To rightly estimate Paisiello's place amid the galaxy of Italian composers is, at the present time, somewhat difficult, especially as so little of his music is nowadays heard. No musician was during his lifetime so universally admired or sought after. Kings and princes clamoured for his services; but success, that 'touchstone of the human character,' never spoiled him.

The music of Paisiello is simple without being insipid, clear and intelligent without lacking ornament and richness of melody, sprightly and bright without being trivial.

He was the first to introduce the viola into comic opera at Naples, and the first to bring concerted bassoons and clarinets into use in both the theatre and churches of Naples.

Paisiello can be majestic, tragic, pathetic, comic, without being heavy, terrific, insipid, or grotesque.

With the name of GIUSEPPE SARTI we may conclude the list of the less-known composers whose songs were sung in old St. Cecilia's. He was born at Faenza in Italy in 1729, and died in Berlin in 1802. In 1756 we find him court-musician at Copenhagen, later at Venice, still later (1779) *maestro di capella* of the Duomo, Milan. At this time his fame was already at its zenith: the Italian theatres clamoured for his operas, his countrymen had named him 'il divino maestro,' and his *Giulio Sabino* was shortly to procure him an invitation to the Russian imperial court. This he accepted in 1785. He at once fell in with the prevailing Russian taste for very noisy music, and is said to have actually introduced into the performance of a 'Te Deum,' in presence of the court, the firing of cannon placed outside the castle. In 1786 the Empress ennobled Sarti and provided for him a most handsome income. He remained eighteen years in St. Petersburg, only quitting it in 1801 by permission of Alexander I. on account of ill health. He was making for the sunnier south when death overtook him in Berlin. Sarti wrote two score or so of *opera buffa*, but amongst his serious operas may be mentioned *Didone* (1767) and *La Clemenza di Tito* (1771). Sarti visited London in 1769.

CHAPTER VI

VARIOUS ACCOUNTS OF THE OLD EDINBURGH CONCERTS

WE shall now search chronologically through contemporary and recent literature for allusions more or less direct to these old concerts, both those in St. Mary's Chapel and those in St. Cecilia's Hall.

I. Allan Ramsay in 'The City of Edinburgh's Address to the Country' (1716) thus alludes to the Musical Club :—

> 'And others can with music make you gay,
> With sweetest sounds Corelli's art display,
> While they around in softest measures sing,
> Or beat melodious solos from the string.'

Allan Ramsay has a poem, 'To the Music Club' (1721), which contains the following lines :—

> . . . . .
>
> 'While vocal tubes and comfort strings engage
> To speak the dialect of the Golden Age,
> Then you, whose symphony of souls proclaim
> Your kin to heav'n, add to your country's fame,

And show that music may have as good fate
In Albion's Glen as Umbria's green retreat,
And with Corelli's soft Italian song,
Mix " Cowdenknowes " and " Winter nights are long."
Nor should the martial Pibroch be despised :
Own'd and refin'd by you, these shall the more be prized,
Each ravished ear extols your heavenly art
Which soothes our care and elevates the heart.'

The following poem is full of local allusions, and is attributed to Allan Ramsay:—

AN EPISTLE TO JAMES OSWALD ON HIS LEAVING EDINBURGH

(From the *Scots Magazine*, October 1741.)

' Dear Oswald, could my verse as sweetly flow
As notes thou softly touchest with the bow,
When all the circling fair attentive hing
On ilk vibration of thy trembling string,
I'd sing how thou wouldst melt our souls away
By solemn notes, or cheer us with the gay,
In verse as lasting as thy tune shall be,
As soft as thy new polish'd " Danton me."
But wha can sing that feels wi' sae great pain
The loss for which Edina sighs in vain?
Our concert now nae mair the ladies mind,
They've a' forgot the gate to Niddery's Wynd ;
Nae mair the " Braes of Ballandine " can charm,
Nae mair can " Fortha's Bank " our bosom warm,
Nae mair the " Northern Lass " attention draw,
Nor " Pinky-house " gi' place to " Alloa."

    .   .   .   .

'Alas! no more shall thy gay tunes delight,
No more thy notes sadness or joy excite,
No more thy solemn bass's awful sound
Shall from the Chapel's vaulted roof rebound.[1]
London, alas! which aye has been our bane,[2]
To which our very loss is certain gain,
 .   .   .   .
If they thy value know as well as we,
Perhaps our vanished gold may flow to thee.'

II. Mackay in his *Journey through Scotland*[3] writes of the concert, and says he was at several 'consorts in Edinburgh,' and declares that he had never seen in any country 'an assembly of greater beauties.' This journey was made in 1723.

Mackay was, apparently, a better judge of good looks than of good music, but he could have been no judge at all of spelling.

III. *Maitland's Account of the Origin of the Musical Society of Edinburgh.*[4]

Maitland is talking of St. Mary's Chapel in the Niddry Wynd:—

'At present it is the hall belonging to the Wrights and Masons, and the upper part is employed by the Musical Society, who hold their weekly concerts therein, of which erection I shall subjoin the following account.

---

[1] St. Mary's Chapel, Niddry Wynd.
[2] This is possibly an allusion to the Union. [3] P. 274.
[4] *History of Edinburgh*, 1753, p. 167.

'Certain gentlemen of this city having in the year 1728 proposed to erect a Musical Society in Edinburgh for the diversion of themselves and friends, the motion was so well approved of that it was readily agreed to by a number of lovers of harmony, who, forming themselves into a fraternity, met and agreed on the following regulations for their better government.

'"At Edinburgh, the 29th March 1728, we, the members of the Musical Society held weekly in Mary's Chapel in Niddry's Wynd, either now subscribing or who shall subscribe on or before the second Wednesday of June next, being resolved for our mutual diversion and entertainment to continue the same and to render it perpetual, have agreed and do hereby agree to assemble ourselves weekly in the said place for the performance of concerts of music as we have already done for these twelve months past, under the following articles and regulations which are hereby declared to be the fundamental laws of the Society to which we do respectfully submit :—

'"(1) That the Society shall consist of a number of members not exceeding seventy, unless it shall afterwards appear necessary in a general meeting to increase the number.

'"(2) That for the preservation of order and the management of the affairs of the Society there shall be a governor, deputy-governor, treasurer, and five directors elected in a general meeting of the subscribers hereby appointed to be held upon the second Wednesday of June next ensuing at five o'clock in the afternoon, in the hall, and afterwards to be annually elected in general meetings of the Society hereby appointed to be held at the same place and at the same hour upon every second Wednesday of June yearly thereafter, and that the said election shall proceed by way of ballot.

'"(3) That upon the second Wednesday of June ensuing, in the said first general meeting and every general meeting yearly thereafter, before proceeding to the election of the said officers of the Society, every member shall pay a guinea into the hands of Mr. Robert Lumisden, our present cashier, or into the hands of the treasurer for the time being, towards defraying the annual charge of the Society and the augmenting its stock.

'"(4) That a book shall be kept wherein shall be recorded the minutes of procedure in the said general meetings, and likewise the matters which shall occur in the ordinary course of administration of the governor and directors, which, being fairly entered into the said book, shall be duly signed by the governor or deputy-governor, and four of the directors hereby appointed to be a quorum.

'"(5) That the Society, being thus regularly constituted with a governor and directors, shall after the said first general meeting proceed to consider the requests of those who desire to be received and admitted as members of the Society, and that the question 'Admit or not' shall be determined in a meeting consisting of the governor or deputy-governor and quorum of directors and fifteen members, by the majority of voices declared after the manner of ballot. That the member admitted shall pay into the hands of the treasurer a guinea to serve as his contribution for that year wherein he enters, and that a record of such admission and payment shall be duly entered into the book of the Society, and signed as aforesaid.

'"(6) And to the end that the yearly contribution of the members may be paid regularly and without trouble to the treasurer, every member neglecting to pay the same as directed by the third article, shall *eo ipso* not only forfeit all right in the Society, and be no longer deemed a member thereof, but is hereby declared to be incapable of being again received as a member upon any after application, unless he shall justify such a cause of admission as excuses him from the apparent contempt, and may induce the Society to admit him anew, according to the fifth article, upon payment of such additional contribution as to the meeting assembled for his re-admission shall seem fit.

'"(7) That a concert of musick shall be performed every *Friday* during the time of session, which shall begin precisely at six o'clock in the afternoon in summer, and at half an hour after five in the winter.

'"(8) That there shall be no dividend made of any money arising from the yearly contributions or otherwise, without the consent of the governor and directors and two-thirds of the members.

'"(9) That it shall belong to the governor and directors to appoint concerts for the entertainment of the ladies at such times as they shall think proper; that the tickets by which the ladies are to be admitted shall be issued by the treasurer, not exceeding the number of sixty (except on the Feast of St. Cecilia), to be purchased from the treasurer by the members of the Society alone, at the rate of half a crown each, upon the Wednesday immediately preceding the concert, and if any are to be returned it shall only be on the day following, before one o'clock in the afternoon.

'"(10) That the management of every matter and thing, whether touching the performance of musick or the execution of the rules and orders of the Society contained either in these articles, or found afterwards convenient to be agreed to for the better government of the Society, shall be the province of the governor and directors.

'"(11) That the treasurer shall fit his accompts yearly

with the governor and directors some time in the month of March.

'"(12) That the governor, deputy-governor, and directors shall have the privilege of inviting one or two of their acquaintances to share of the musick performed in the said concerts other than those to which ladies happen to be invited, to which none but members are to be admitted, unless in some very particular case it shall appear reasonable to the governor and directors to allow of the same."'

Maitland continues:—'The above contract and articles are subscribed by the seventy members aforesaid. This Society was so highly approved of, that many persons of distinction applied to be admitted members. But the place of meeting not being capacious enough to admit a great number, a few years after the erection of the Society, thirty persons were admitted, whereby the members were increased to one hundred in number, who continue to meet as aforesaid to divert themselves and friends in the most agreeable and delightful manner with both vocal and instrumental musick by a number of the best performers.'[1]

Such is Maitland's account of the origin of an essentially amateur society, destined to wield by its distinguished patronage a most important influence over Scottish music to the end of the eighteenth century.

[1] *History of Edinburgh*, p. 168.

Various Accounts of the Concerts 199

By the kindness of Mr. R. A. Marr, C.A., the well-known historian of the rise of choral societies in Scotland, we are enabled to publish a complete list of the members of the Musical Society of Edinburgh at a time when its constitution may be taken as quite typical (1775).

Mr. Marr, in sending us this very rare pamphlet, writes:—'The list as a record of names prominent in Edinburgh society of that period is a very complete and useful one.'

We reproduce it as Appendix No. III.

IV. *Dr. Tobias Smollett on the Edinburgh Concert* (1756).

There is, indeed, no elaborate reference in *Humphry Clinker* to the Musical Society of Edinburgh, but a quite unequivocal allusion to it occurring in one of the letters from Edinburgh is interesting.

It is dated 'Edinburgh, August 8th,' and 1756 is, as we know from other sources, the date of Smollett's visit: it is addressed to 'Sir Watkin Phillips, Bart., of Jesus College, Oxon,' and contains the following:—

'All the diversions of London we enjoy at Edinburgh in a small compass. Here is a well-conducted *Concert*, in which several gentlemen perform on different instruments. The Scots are all musicians. Every man you meet plays on the flute, the violin, or the violoncello, and there is one nobleman whose compositions are universally admired.[1]

'Our company of actors is very tolerable, and a subscription is now afoot for building a theatre, but their assemblies please me above all other public exhibitions.'

V. *The Account in Defoe's 'Tour Through Great Britain.'*

Daniel Defoe, sent to Scotland by Godolphin to further secretly or by any means in his power the union between England and Scotland, resided in Edinburgh on several occasions between 1706 and 1712. Defoe died in London on the 26th of April 1731, thirty-one years before St. Cecilia's Hall was built, and yet there is an allusion to it in a work associated with Defoe's name, the title of which is '*A Tour through the whole Island of Great Britain*, originally begun by the celebrated Daniel Defoe, continued by the late Mr. Richardson, author of *Clarissa*, and brought down to the present time by a gentleman of eminence in the literary world.' Four volumes, London, 1769.

Leslie Stephen in his life of Defoe[2] gives the date of Defoe's 'Tour' as 1724 to 1726, so that it is quite clear the description of the hall is not by Defoe, but probably

---

[1] This is Lord Kelly.
[2] *Dictionary of National Biography.*

Various Accounts of the Concerts

by the 'gentleman of eminence in the literary world.' It occurs in a letter dated 1768, and is as follows:—

'The new concert-hall (built about three years ago) is an elegant room of an elliptical form, with a concave ceiling and a large skylight in the centre. From the ceiling depend seven handsome branches filled with wax lights. It is most commodiously fitted up with seats rising gradually above each other, and seems (upon the whole) one of the best calculated rooms for music that is (perhaps) to be met with in Britain. The roof, however, is thought to be rather too low, and the room is more warm than is agreeable in summer.'

VI. *Captain Topham's Account.*

The following is from the *Letters from Edinburgh* of a Captain Topham, an Englishman who resided in Edinburgh in 1774 and 1775 for a period of six months. He writes:—

'One of the principal entertainments in Edinburgh is a concert which is supported by subscription, and under the direction of a governor, deputy-governor, treasurer, and five directors, who procure some of the best performers from other countries, and have a weekly concert in an elegant room which they have built for that purpose, and which is styled St. Cecilia's Hall. It is rather too confined, but in every other respect the best accommodated to music of any room I ever was in. The figure of it is elliptical, and the roof is vaulted, and a single instrument is heard in it with the greatest possible advantage. The managers of the concert have a certain number of tickets to distribute to their friends, so that none are admitted but the people of fashion.

'Though the band is a good one in general, yet I cannot say much of the vocal performers. The natives of this country are not remarkable for their abilities in singing, and except in a few of the real Scotch tunes, I have never met with a voice that had either compass or an agreeable tone. But in order to make up this deficiency in their own countrymen, the managers take care to have some of the best singers from London and Italy.

'At present they have some tolerably good ones, who are not quite so admired as a Gabrielli or a Tenducci would be,—the latter of whom, before he fled from Great Britain, resided here a considerable time, and was one cause of introducing that rage for Italian music which is now so predominant.

'Indeed, the degree of attachment which is shown to music in general in this country exceeds belief. It is not only the principal entertainment, but the constant topic of every conversation; and it is necessary not only to be a lover of it, but to be possessed of a knowledge of the science, to make yourself agreeable to society. In vain may a man of letters, whose want of natural faculties has prevented him from understanding an art from which he could derive no pleasure, endeavour to introduce other matters of discourse, however entertaining in their nature: everything must give place to music.

'Music alone engrosses every idea. In religion a Scotchman is grave and abstracted, in politics serious and deliberate: it is in the power of harmony alone to make him an enthusiast. What a misfortune it is to the country, and how trifling does it appear to a stranger, to find so many philosophers, professors of science, and respectable characters disputing on the merits of an Italian fiddle and the preciseness of a demi-quaver, while poetry, painting, architecture, and theatrical amusements, whose province it is to instruct as well as to amuse, here couch beneath the dominion of an air or a ballad, which at best were only invented to pass away a vacant hour or ease the mind from more important duties.'

VII. *Hugo Arnot's Account.*[1]

We give it in full:—

'*Of the Concert.*—The Musical Society of Edinburgh, whose weekly concerts form one of the most elegant entertainments of that metropolis, was first instituted in the year 1728.

[1] Arnot, *History of Edinburgh*, 1779.

'Before that time several gentlemen, performers on the harpsichord and violin, had formed a weekly club at the Cross Keys tavern (kept by one Steil, a great lover of musick and a good singer of Scots songs), where the common entertainment consisted in playing the concertos and sonatas of Corelli, then just published, and the overtures of Handel.

'That meeting becoming numerous, they instituted in March 1728 a society of seventy members, for the purpose of holding a weekly concert. A governor, deputy-governor, treasurer, and five directors are annually chosen by the members for regulating the affairs of this Society. Its meetings have been continued since that period much on the same plan, only the place where they are held has been changed from St. Mary's Chapel to their own hall. These meetings are only interrupted during three or four weeks of the vacation, in the months of September and October.

'The present concert-hall, which is situated in a centrical part of the town, was built A.D. 1762. The plan was drawn by Sir Robert Mylne, architect of Blackfriars-bridge, after the model of the great opera-theatre at Parma, but on a smaller scale, and the expense was defrayed by voluntary subscription among the members.

'The musical room is reckoned uncommonly elegant. It is of an oval form, the ceiling a concave elliptical

Various Accounts of the Concerts 205

dome, lighted solely from the top by a lanthorn. Its construction is excellently adapted for music; and the seats ranged in the room in the form of an amphitheatre, besides leaving a large area in the middle of the room, are capable of containing a company of about five hundred persons. The orchestre is at the upper end, which is handsomely terminated by an elegant organ.

'The band consists of a *maestro di capella*, an organist, two violins, two tenors, six or eight *ripienos*, a double or *contra* base, and harpsichord; and occasionally two French horns, besides kettledrums, flutes, and clarinets. There is always one good singer, and there are sometimes two, upon the establishment.

'A few years ago the celebrated Tenducci was at the head of this company. The principal foreign masters at present in the service of the Musical Society are: first violin, Signor Puppo; second, Signor Corri; violoncello, Schetky; singers, Signor and Signora Corri. All of these are excellent in their different apartments. They have salaries from the Society according to their respective merits.

'Besides an ordinary concert in honour of St. Cecilia, the patroness of music, there are usually performed in the course of the year two or three of Handel's oratorios. That great master gave this Society the privilege of having full copies made for them of all his manuscript oratorios.

'An occasional concert is sometimes given upon the death of a governor or director. This is conducted in the manner of a *concerto spirituale*. The pieces are of sacred music, the symphonies accompanied with the full organ, French horns, clarinets, kettledrums. Upon these occasions the audience is in deep mourning, which, added to the pathetic solemnity of the music, has a noble and striking effect upon the mind.' (One of these funeral concerts—which have certainly no present-day equivalent—we have alluded to on p. 154. This was the one in memory of Lord Drummore, given on the 27th of June 1755, the whole company being dressed in the deepest mourning. By the kindness of Mr. Marr we have been enabled to reproduce the title-page of the programme, or, as we would now say, 'book of words,' issued for this funeral concert, which precious relic is part of Mr. Marr's valuable musical collection.)

'The music generally performed is a proper mixture of the modern and ancient style. The former, although agreeable to the prevailing taste, is not allowed to debar the amusement of those who find more pleasure in the old compositions. In every plan there are one or two pieces of Corelli, Handel, or Geminiani.

'Among the number of members, which is now increased to two hundred, there are many excellent performers who take their parts in the orchestra especially in extraordinary concerts, where sometimes

FUNERAL CONCERT

Performed by

The GENTLEMEN of

THE

MUSICAL SOCIETY,

Of EDINBURGH,

On the DEATH of

The Lord DRUMMORE,

Their GOVERNOR.

27th JUNE, M.DCC.LV.

a whole act is performed solely by the gentlemen-members.

'Formerly some of the members of this Society instituted a catch-club which met after the concert. On the great concert in honour of St. Cecilia the governor and directors were in use to invite a few of their friends and strangers of fashion to an entertainment of this kind after the concert, where select pieces of vocal music were performed intermingled with Scots songs, duets, catches, and glees. There were many excellent voices in the catch-club who sung each their part at sight, and the easy cheerfulness which reigned in this select society rendered their meetings delightful.

'When the Prince of Hesse was in Scotland in 1745-46, his Highness and several of the nobility were elegantly entertained by Lord Drummore, then Governor of the Musical Society, and the gentlemen of the catch-club. The prince was not only a dilettante, but a good performer on the violoncello. The Scots songs and English catches were to him a new and an agreeable entertainment.

'The selection of company which for some years gave high spirit and repute to this joyous and convivial club by degrees relaxed: it of course became numerous and expensive, and at last broke up.

'Company are admitted to the entertainments of the

concert by special tickets which are not transferable, which serve for the night only upon which they are granted; and in the admission, which is always gratis, except at the benefit concerts given for the emolument of performers, a preference is constantly shown to strangers.

'By a uniform adherence to the spirit and rules of the Society, and strict economy in the management of their funds, the Musical Society has subsisted these fifty years with great honour and reputation, and at present it is esteemed one of the most elegant and genteel entertainments conducted upon the most moderate expense of any in Britain.'

In the appendix to his *History*, Arnot says that in 1763 the concert began at six o'clock in the evening, and in 1783 at seven o'clock: finally a compromise was made, and 6.30 was the hour fixed on. Arnot writes:—'The barbarous custom of "saving the ladies," as it was called, after St. Cecilia's concerts, by the gentlemen drinking immoderately to "save" his favourite lady, is now given up—indeed they got no thanks for their absurdity.'

Chambers describes this custom. It was merely a particular form of toast-drinking in which a man, challenged as to the charms of his 'lady,' drank deeper to her in the next toast, and so 'saved' her (by damning himself, as our friends the teetotalers would tell us).

Various Accounts of the Concerts

VIII. *Kincaid's Account of the Hall.*

Kincaid, the well-known Edinburgh printer of Bibles —as printer to the King in Scotland—has left us a brief, but not wholly accurate, account of St. Cecilia's. He wrote in 1787, and his words are :—

'*Concert Hall.*—This, otherwise called St. Cecilia's Hall, was built in 1762 under the direction of Sir Robert Mylne, architect of Blackfriars Bridge, after the model of the opera-theatre of Parma. The building stands on the east side of Niddry's Wynd, near the Cowgate, and will now be close by the same side of the South Bridge. The room is excellently adapted for music, being oval, having a concave ceiling of the same form; the seats are ranged round the room in such a manner as to leave a large area in the middle. The orchestra is at one end, and has an elegant organ.'

IX. The following description is also attributed to Kincaid :—

'It was designed after the model of the opera-theatre at Parma. The room is excellently adapted for music, being oval, having a concave ceiling of the same form; the seats are ranged round the room in such a manner as to leave a large area in the middle. It only remains to add that the sole light of the hall is from a comparatively small oval light in the centre of the oval ceiling, like the single eye of a cyclops.

'The amount of light introduced into the room by this one vertical light, like the Pantheon at Rome, is remarkable. It is impossible to contemplate this room without concluding that he was an artistic and original man who designed it.'

X. In a work published in 1829, dedicated to Sir Walter Scott, Bart., and possessed of the following ponderous title—'*Modern Athens, displayed in a Series of Views:* or Edinburgh in the Nineteenth Century, exhibiting the whole of the modern improvements, antiquities, and picturesque scenery of the Scottish Metropolis and its Environs, from original drawings by Mr. Thomas H. Shepherd, with historical, topographical, and critical illustrations'[1]—St. Cecilia's Hall is thus briefly alluded to :—

'In 1728 a Musical Society was instituted in Edinburgh for weekly concerts, and this not only gave encouragement to the science, but created amateurs and professors. At first this Society assembled in St. Mary's Chapel, but increasing in number and property, "The Gentleman's Concert," as then called, built a hall in 1762 in imitation of the opera-theatre at Paris. Mr. Robert Mylne, the architect of Blackfriars Bridge,

[1] London : Jones and Co., Finsbury Square, 1829.

Various Accounts of the Concerts

London, was engaged to design the building. The great music-room was of an oval shape, lighted from the centre of a concave elliptical dome, and the seats were arranged amphitheatrically to accommodate an auditory of about five hundred persons. For some years this was a strictly private society, and visitors were admitted by complimentary tickets.' (It would be charitable to believe that 'Paris' is a misprint for 'Parma': Peebles would have been quite as near the truth.)

XI. *Lord Cockburn on St. Cecilia's Hall.*[1]

'For example, St. Cecilia's Hall was the only public resort of the musical, and besides being our most selectly fashionable place of amusement, was the best and most beautiful concert-room I have ever yet seen, and there have I myself seen most of our literary and fashionable gentlemen predominating with their side-curls and frills and ruffles and silver buckles; and our stately matrons stiffened in hoops and gorgeous satin, and our beauties with high-heeled shoes, powdered and pomatomed hair, and lofty and composite head-dresses, —all this in the Cowgate, the last retreat nowadays of destitution and disease. The building still stands, though raised and changed, and is looked down upon from the South Bridge, over the eastern side of the

[1] *Memorials of My Time*, p. 29.

Cowgate arch. When I last saw it, it seemed to be partly an old clothesman's shop and partly a brazier's.'

In the *Journal*,[1] when enumerating the places of entertainment in Edinburgh in the end of last century, Lord Cockburn says :—'St. Cecilia's Hall, the concert-room in the Cowgate, which, when it was built in 1762, deserved the praise of Arnot for being "situated in a centrical part of the town,"' etc. etc.

In Grant's *Old and New Edinburgh*[2] the description is substantially that by Arnot and by George Thomson: the former we have quoted verbatim, and the latter we now proceed similarly to reproduce.

XII. George Thomson thus describes the scene of many of his happiest hours :—

'The concerts of St. Cecilia's Hall formed one of the most liberal and attractive amusements that any city in Europe could boast of. The hall was built on purpose at the foot of Niddry's Wynd by a number of public-spirited noblemen and gentlemen, and the expense of the concerts was defrayed by about two hundred subscribers paying two or three guineas each annually; and so respectable was the institution considered, that upon the death of a member there were generally several applications for the vacancy, as is now the case

---

[1] A continuation of the *Memorials*, p. 196.
[2] Cassell and Co.

Various Accounts of the Concerts 215

with the Caledonian Hunt. The concerts were managed by a governor and a set of six or more directors, who engaged the performers—the principal ones from Italy, one or two from Germany, and the rest of the orchestra was made up of English and native artists.

'The concerts were given weekly during most of the time that I attended, the instrumental music consisting chiefly of the concertos of Corelli and Handel and the overtures of Bach, Abel, Stamitz, Vanhall, and latterly of Haydn and Pleyel; for at that time, and till a good many years after, the magnificent symphonies of Haydn, Mozart, and Beethoven, which now form the most attractive portions of all public concerts, had not reached this country. Those truly grand symphonies do not seem likely to be superseded by any similar compositions for a century to come, transcending so immensely as they do all the orchestral compositions that ever before appeared. Yet I must not venture to prophesy, when I bear in mind what a powerful influence fashion and folly exercise upon music as well as upon other objects of taste.

'When the overtures and quartetts of Haydn first found their way into this country, I well remember with what coldness the former were received by most of the grave Handelians, while at the theatres they gave delight. . . .

'The vocal department of our concerts consisted

chiefly of the songs of Handel, Arne, Gluck, Sarti, Jornelli, Guglielmi, Paisiello, Scottish songs, etc.; and every year generally we had an oratorio of Handel performed with the assistance of a principal bass and a tenor singer and a few chorus singers from the English Cathedrals, together with some Edinburgh amateurs who cultivated that sacred and sublime music, Signor and Signora Domenico Corri, the latter our prima donna, singing most of the principal songs or most interesting portion of the music. On such occasions the hall was always crowded to excess by a splendid assemblage including all the beauty and fashion of our city.

'A supper to the directors and their friends at Fortune's Tavern generally followed the oratorio, where the names of the chief beauties who had graced the hall were honoured by their healths being drunk....

'The hall, built in 1762 from a design of Mr. Robert Milne after the model of the great opera-theatre of Parma, was an exact oval, having a concave elliptical ceiling, and was remarkable for the clear and perfect conveyance of sounds without responding echoes, as well as for the judicious manner in which the seating was arranged. In this last respect, I have seen no concert-room equal to it either in London or Paris.

'The orchestra was erected at the upper end of the hall opposite to the door of entrance; a portion of the

Various Accounts of the Concerts

area in the centre or widest part was without any seats, and served as a small promenade where friends could chat together during the interval of performance. The seats were all *fixed* down on both sides of the hall, and each side was raised by a gradual elevation from the level area backward, the rows of seats behind each other, till they reached a passage a few feet broad that was carried quite round the hall behind the last of the elevated seats;[1] so that when the audience was seated each half of it fronted the other—an arrangement much preferable to that commonly adopted of placing all the seats upon a level behind each other, for thus the whole company must look one way and see each other's backs.

'A private staircase at the upper end of the hall, not seen by the company, admitted the musicians into the orchestra, in the front of which stood a harpsichord with the singers and the principal violoncellist, and behind these, on a platform a little elevated, were the violins and other stringed and wind instruments, just behind which stood a noble organ. The hall when filled contained an audience of about four hundred. No money was taken for admission, tickets being given gratis to the lovers of music and to strangers.'

XIII. Sir Daniel Wilson, in the last edition (1891)

[1] See page 31 for the illustration of this arrangement.

of his *Memorials of Edinburgh in the Olden Time*, thus speaks of St. Cecilia's :—

'Only six years before the commencement of the works beyond the North Loch, Sir Robert Mylne was employed to furnish the designs for St. Cecilia's Hall in the Cowgate. It was built after the model of the great Theatre Farnese at Parma, and though now long deserted by the votaries of St. Cecilia, it was admirably adapted for the purposes of a concert-room, its oval form and elliptical ceiling, as well as the skilful arrangement of the seats, uniting to convey every note clearly and distinctly to the auditors. In this respect the great Music Hall of the New Town is decidedly inferior, notwithstanding the lapse of above eighty years since the building of St. Cecilia's Hall, and the great attention devoted in the interval to the practical application of acoustics in architecture.'

Such are the descriptions of these bygone concerts; but it must not be imagined that the old hall was used for no other purpose than for the concerts of the 'Musical Society of Edinburgh.'

A study of old Edinburgh records clearly shows that St. Cecilia's Hall in the Niddry Wynd, although the property of the governors and directors, was used for the following different kinds of concert or gathering :—

1. The St. Cecilia Concert of the Musical Society,

usually on a Friday evening at 6 P.M.[1] To this concert the public, as such, were not admitted; the members needed no tickets, they went *ex officiis*, but each member (and all! the members were men—see Appendix III.) could obtain ladies' tickets by applying for them personally or by written order.

Any member of the Musical Society could introduce a guest of his own or some distinguished person visiting the town.

Such an announcement as the following has reference to this regular and, as it were, statutory concert of the great amateur society :—

Edinburgh Evening Courant, February 13th, 1768.

'The gentlemen of the Musical Society have appointed St. Cecilia's Concert to be held on Friday, 19th inst., beginning at six o'clock in the evening. The members will please call for ladies' tickets at the usual place on Thursday.'

2. A concert held on some special occasion either to honour some individual or in commemoration of some high office-bearer in the Musical Society—as, for instance, that on St. Cecilia's Day, November 22nd, or a funeral concert.

3. An oratorio, usually of Handel's : thus *Edinburgh Evening Courant*, July 30th, 1768 :—'The gentlemen

[1] During 1768 and 1769 the hour was 6 P.M.

of the Musical Society have appointed an Oratorio to be performed on Friday, 15th August next, in St. Cecilia's Hall. The members will please to call on Thursday for tickets at the usual place. Each member can only have two ladies' tickets, and none will be given out but to a member himself or to his signed order.'

4. Concerts 'by order' of the governors and directors of the Musical Society—for instance, a concert of Tenducci's on February 28th, 1769. These were concerts arranged by some musician, and the other professional musicians who took part did so as engaged by him, and not as officially belonging to the orchestra or in the pay of the Musical Society.

5. Benefit concerts for some distinguished professional musician. These were either 'by authority' or 'by permission' of the governors and directors of the Musical Society.

6. Concerts 'by particular desire of several persons of distinction,' who may or may not have been members of the Musical Society—for instance, Tenducci's on May 25th, 1768. This may be looked on as a St. Cecilia concert to which the *public* were admitted.

7. Concerts got up by some individual and held in St. Cecilia's Hall, in the announcements of which there is no mention whatever of the Musical Society. The

Various Accounts of the Concerts

use of the hall, probably rented, must have been privately arranged for by the musician giving the concert.

As examples of this class of concert :—

Edinburgh Evening Courant, January 9th, 1768.

'On Tuesday, 26th inst., Signor Arrigoni's concert will be given in St. Cecilia's Hall, Niddry's Wynd. Tickets 2s. 6d., at Bremner's music-shop. To commence at 5 P.M.'

And the following :—

'On December 17th, 1768, Mr. Gilson's vocal and instrumental concert in St. Cecilia's Hall is announced for December 20th. Tickets 2s. 6d., at Balfour's coffee-house and Bremner's music-shop.'

For concerts of classes three to seven the public could purchase tickets.

At some of these concerts many, probably all, the artistes in the town at the time would contribute something, as at 'Mr. Thomson's Concert,' advertised on January 4th, 1769, when Tenducci, Madame Doria, and Mr. Gilson all assisted as vocalists, and when an overture by Lord Kelly, with clarionets, hautbois, German flutes, French horns, and kettledrums, was performed.

8. An occasional lecture, it would seem, was given

in the old concert-hall, just as nowadays a concert-room is sometimes used for purposes other than musical. The *Edinburgh Evening Courant* of March 27th, 1769, announces:—'By particular permission, on Thursday, 30th March inst., Mr. Stayley will deliver a public lecture on the Art of Reading, with several pieces of music by the Principle (*sic*) performers, at 7 P.M. Tickets 2s. 6d.'

9. Meetings of the 'Ladies' Academy': to this the following refers:—*Edinburgh Evening Courant*, November 21st, 1768:—'On Monday next will be the second meeting of the Ladies' Academy at St. Cecilia's, and by desire of the governess will begin precisely at 12 o'clock. Subscribers' tickets to be got of Mr. Tenducci. The next tickets are red, and no other tickets will be admitted but of that colour.'

Anything relating to the musical instruments of the place we welcome, especially after so long an interval. The organ mentioned several times by contemporary writers is thus alluded to by Sir John Graham Dalzell in his book on music in Scotland:[1]—

'There was an organ in the Concert Hall in 1765, whereon, at the benefit of Doria, that musician was to perform a solo with a pastorale. An organ reckoned

---

[1] *Musical Memoirs of Scotland*, with historical annotations and numerous illustrative plates, by Sir John Graham Dalzell, Knight and Baronet, 1849, p. 132.

good in its time served many years there for performances: it was transferred to the Assembly Rooms, George Street, about the year 1800, and it was finally taken down to be employed, as far as might be, in other instruments seven or eight years ago.'

CHAPTER VII

THE AUDIENCE

THE period at which St. Cecilia concerts would be in the zenith of their success was just about the time that Robert Burns paid his first visit to Edinburgh upon the invitation of that genial man of letters, the blind Dr. Blacklock, whose kindly letter to Burns on the eve of his sailing for Jamaica was not only the first streak of light upon poor Burns's horizon, but, all unconscious as it was to Blacklock, the means also of preserving from premature extinction the brightest light that ever glowed in the Temple of the Scottish Muses.

It was in the year 1786, upon November the 28th, in the evening, that 'that bright particular star' housed itself in Mrs. Carfrae's lodgings in Baxter's Close on the north side of the Lawnmarket, on the ground-floor of a house whose windows looked into Lady Stair's Close. We like to be precise in such matters, for it was from this particular spot on the earth's surface that that light—fired by the splendid enthusiasm of the warmth of unsophisticated nature—went nightly forth to carry its healthy brilliance into the more artificially illuminated circle of a society which was one of the most cultured, critical, and philosophical to be found at that time in any European capital.

From the Anchor Close and 'Creech's Land' went forth much of the best in literature and a very large proportion of all British publication, while the Old Edinburgh drawing-rooms, filled with cultured beauties, echoed to learned repartee and elegant wit.

Literary and academic as she was, Edinburgh was yet to experience the honour of being made as famous in the wider world of letters as ever Athens, Alexandria, or Paris had been; for was she not maturing Scott—that little lame boy of fourteen or fifteen, who was to meet Burns, that famous *once*, at Professor Ferguson's in Old Sciennes House, and to receive from those wonderful eyes that smile of thanks to be cherished for evermore?

From Mr. Martin Hardie's picture, ' Burns reciting his Poem, "A Winter's Night," at the Duchess of Gordon's,' we get an excellent idea of one of these literary gatherings of which we are speaking. The artist has represented the scene as taking place in the beautiful wall-painted drawing-room of Lord Glenlee's town house (then 17 Brown Square, now 31 Chambers Street), although the probability is it occurred in the

Gordon mansion on the Castle Hill. The group is quite typical, for there are present:—

> Jane, fourth Duchess of Gordon (the hostess).
> The Dowager-Countess of Glencairn, and her son the Earl of Glencairn.
> Lord Monboddo (James Burnet) and Miss Elizabeth Burnet, his second daughter.
> Miss Margaret Chalmers ('Peggy').
> The Rev. Dr. Blacklock.
> Henry Mackenzie ('The Man of Feeling').
> The Rev. Dr. Hugh Blair, F.R.S.E.
> Professor Dugald Stewart (Moral Philosophy).
> The Hon. Henry Erskine (third son of the tenth Earl of Buchan)—'Harry Erskine.'
> Old Professor Adam Ferguson.
> William Tytler, William Creech (Provost and publisher), and Alexander Nasmyth the painter.

About most of them Burns had something characteristic to say.

The owner of the house, 17 Brown Square, was made Lord President in 1788, and in 1789, the year of his death, was created a baronet, Sir Thomas Miller of Glenlee. His wife, formerly Miss Chalmers of Pittencrief, was one of the Edinburgh beauties to be seen at the St. Cecilia concerts.

We shall begin with Miss Burnet of Monboddo, who

must have been one of the most lovely girls of her own or any other time. Burns, shortly after his arrival in the city, and writing in that dark old Lawnmarket house, recognises her as one of the features of Edina itself, for he says in the 'Address to Edinburgh':—

> 'Thy daughters bright thy walks adorn,
>   Gay as the gilded summer sky,
> Sweet as the dewy milk-white thorn,
>   Dear as the raptured thrill of joy!
> Fair Burnet strikes th' adoring eye,
>   Heaven's beauties on my fancy shine;
> I see the Sire of Love on high,
>   And own his work indeed divine.'

No small honour to have been ranked by Scotland's greatest poet as one of the features of beauty in a scene where all is beauty.

We make no apology whatever for considering that we shall best describe the St. Cecilia audience by describing only its ladies, or rather allowing Burns, so sympathetic an authority, to do so, seeing that *they* it is who constitute 'society,' the gentlemen being merely —from an æsthetic point of view—the background to show up the tones and outlines of the picture.

The position of the gentlemen reminds us of a bridegroom on his wedding-day—a person so completely lost sight of that he might be not unjustly defined as the indispensable but unimportant condition wtihout which the ceremony could not be legalised, or, if you will, a mere 'accessory before the fact.'

It is not that Burns has nothing to say upon the gentlemen: he has. There are two poems on Glencairn, an address to William Tytler of Woodhouselee, an exquisite piece of satire on Creech, and there are lines on Harry Erskine; but we shall rather hear him on a theme—'The Ladies'—a theme the celebration of which cost him much ink and too often a sacrifice of his normal degree of both physical and mental equilibrium.

It being understood that most of the men of 'light and leading' of their day patronised these concerts, we shall let Burns continue his praise of 'the heavenly Miss Burnet,' to whom 'there has not been anything nearly like ... in all the combinations of beauty, grace, and goodness (which) the Great Creator has formed since Milton's Eve on the first day of her existence.' On hearing of her death, June 17th, 1790, Burns wrote one of the tenderest and intensest of all his elegies: it is all beautiful; we can quote but one stanza:—

> 'We saw thee shine in youth and beauty's pride,
> And virtue's light, that beams beyond the spheres;
> But like the sun eclipsed at morning-tide,
> Thou left'st us darkling in a world of tears.'

This beautiful creature did not long grace Edina's streets, for Old Scotland's wind proving, in her case, much more unkind than man, she went out for milder air to the Braid Farm on the southern uplands of that name, and died there of the fell 'consumption' at the early age of twenty-two years.

Old Mrs. Cockburn, herself a poetess, of 'The Flowers of the Forest' fame, thus wrote of Burns's visit :—' He has seen (the) Duchess of Gordon and all the gay world. His favourite for looks and manners is Bess Burnet—no bad judge indeed.' This was the same old lady who had been a friend of David Hume, and the same who was read to by young Walter Scott, aged seven years—a little boy in his father's house at 25 George Square. It is curious that she and Dr. Blacklock lie buried within a few yards of each other in the almost totally forgotten little burying-ground of the chapel-of-ease of St. Cuthbert's in Buccleuch Street.

The Duchess of Gordon was born Jane Maxwell, second daughter of Sir James and Lady Maxwell of Monreith, Wigtonshire, and she and her younger sister Eglantine (or Eglintoune, for her name was later on changed to Eglintoune owing to her resemblance to the handsome Susannah, Countess of Eglinton) were at this time two of the most beautiful girls in all Scotland.

The family resided in Hyndford's Close (on the south side of the High Street), and the ease of the girls' manners is graphically described by Robert

Chambers in his *Traditions of Edinburgh*, in which occurs the probably not apocryphal story of her future Grace of Gordon riding on a sow's back in the manner, we are to understand, that is advocated by Lady Florence Dixie. This sow is as integral a part of Old Edinburgh legend as is Balaam's ass in its own place. Jane became Duchess of Gordon in 1767; her elder sister, Catherine, Mrs. Fordyce of Aytoun; while the youngest, Eglantine, ere long found herself Lady Wallace of Craigie, whose repartee, grace, abandon, *bonne camaraderie*, have almost passed into a proverb in Edinburgh annals. These three Graces when in Edinburgh for 'the season' were fervent in their patronage of the St. Cecilia concerts.

This Duchess of Gordon, there can be no doubt whatever, was one of the most brilliant, versatile, and socially charming women in the gay throng over which she reigned. The late Professor Blackie in his short *Life of Burns*[1] thus speaks of her:—'The Duchess of Gordon, who figures . . . as an avowed patroness of the poet, seems to have been a person peculiarly fitted for performing that function; . . . with her good sense and her light heart she was ready to take the lead in all the gaieties of the season.'

Burns has not indeed left a poem dedicated to this lady, but he has given us three very pretty stanzas in

[1] Page 78.

praise of her Grace's northern home, 'Castle Gordon.' In his 'Journal,' under date September 7th, 1787, we find the following :—'. . . The Duke makes me happier than ever great man did—noble, princely, yet mild, condescending and affable, gay and kind; the Duchess charming, witty, and sensible,—God bless them.' It was meet that a 'gay Gordon' should marry a still gayer Maxwell.

Before passing on to allow Burns to describe the ladies in the audience of St. Cecilia's, we must note his tribute to a nobleman to whom he was probably more indebted than to any other person for his kind reception in Edinburgh—James Cunningham, fourteenth Earl of Glencairn, himself also an Ayrshire man. Burns has two poems—one, 'Verses intended to be written below a noble Earl's Picture,' which opens with 'Whose is that noble, dauntless brow'; the other a peculiarly sad 'Lament for James, Earl of Glencairn,' which closes with the well-known lines :—

> 'The mother may forget the child
> That smiles sae sweetly on her knee,
> But I'll remember thee, Glencairn,
> And a' that thou hast done for me.'

The noble patron was repaid in noble verse. Lord Glencairn died on 27th January 1791, and Burns attended his funeral at Kilmaurs. He came of a race long ennobled and famous in Scottish history, and was succeeded by his only brother, the Rev. and Hon. John Cunningham, as fifteenth Earl, with whom the title became extinct in 1796, the year Burns died.

Another beauty who attended these old concerts was Margaret Chalmers ('Peggy'), who became Mrs. Lewis Hay, a cousin of Charlotte Hamilton (afterwards Mrs. Adair), a sister of Gavin Hamilton of Mauchline, a very early friend of Burns. While at Harvieston in Clackmannan, Burns met both these girls, and in praise of Charlotte wrote the song, 'The Banks of the Devon,' while Peggy Chalmers was the subject of two poems, one of which ends with the intense couplet:—

> 'But tearing Peggy from my soul
> Must be a stronger death';

the other opening with :—

> 'My Peggy's face, my Peggy's form,
> The frost of hermit age might warm;
> My Peggy's worth, my Peggy's mind,
> Might charm the first of human kind.'

It is interesting to know that, as a matter of fact, the last poem he wrote (dated '12th July 1796'—he died on the 21st) was to the 'Fairest Maid on Devon Banks'; and although there were two 'Maids' who might lay claim to the superlative, there is indirect evidence to show that it was to the lively Peggy rather than to the stately Charlotte that the poet's painfully sensitive soul was turning in its last hours on earth.

As a widow, Mrs. Hay is reported to have told the poet Campbell during his Edinburgh visit that Burns made her a serious proposal of marriage. Those best versed in the extensive subject of Burns's amourology believe that, although he admired the 'divine Burnet,' praised the beautiful Charlotte Hamilton, it was Peggy Chalmers whom he really *loved*.

In a poem of sixteen lines we have the pronoun of appropriation used six times, thus :—

My Peggy's . . . { Face / Form / Worth / Mind / Angel air / Heart }

and the description closes with 'immortal charms.' We are thus justified in believing that Margaret Chalmers had a very narrow escape from being Mrs. Burns.

Another well-known lady of the St. Cecilia concerts was Euphemia Murray of Lintrose, known as the 'Flower of Strathmore,' who married David Smythe of Methven —a Lord of Session, Lord Methven.[1] Of her Burns says that she was—

'Blythe by the banks of Earn,
And blythe in Glenturrit glen,'

which is quite possible, seeing that she was a cousin of Sir William Murray of Ochtertyre—a lovely place

[1] Both buried in the Canongate Churchyard.

covered with exquisite woods, lying between the River Earn and Loch Turrit. Burns further declares that—

> 'Phemie was a bonnier lass
>   Than Braes o' Yarrow ever saw.
> Her looks were like a flower in May,
>   Her smile was like a simmer morn,
> She tripped by the banks o' Earn
>   As light's a bird upon a thorn.'

Mrs. Smythe, when an old lady, told a friend of hers that she remembered 'Burns reciting the poem "Upon scaring Wild-fowl" one evening after supper, and that he pronounced the concluding lines with great energy.' In the Thomson letter (No. XVIII.), dated October 19th, 1794, Burns says of the song, 'Andrew and his cutty gun':—'The song to which this is set in the *Museum* is mine, and was composed on Miss Euphemia Murray of Lintrose, commonly and deservedly called "The Flower of Strathmore."'

Another lady almost certainly present at the concerts in the Niddry Wynd was Mrs. Riddell of Woodley Park, Dumfries. To her Burns writes the 'Complimentary Epigram on Maria Riddell' which has these lines:—

> 'But thee, whom all my soul adores,
>   E'en flattery cannot flatter;
> Maria, all my thought and dream,
>   Inspires my vocal shell:
> The more I praise my lovely theme,
>   The more the truth I tell.'

During Mr. Riddell's absence in the West Indies in 1794, Burns and Mrs. Riddell saw a good deal of each other; but the friendship came to a sudden and violent end in consequence of a drunken practical joke perpetrated upon the ladies of the party at Woodley Park after a dinner given on Mr. Riddell's return to the head of his house and the foot of his table. The men, who were all more or less intoxicated, seem to have agreed to invade the drawing-room in a body, and re-enact, on a small scale, the classic scene of the 'Rape of the Sabines.' Burns, on entering the drawing-room, staggered up to his hostess and kissed her with all the sonorous energy of a bucolic lover—a piece of realism which was too much for Mr. Riddell's philistinism, and far too public a rehearsal of what might conceivably have been privately permitted a year previously. It is almost certainly to Mrs. Riddell that Burns writes the 'Remorseful Apology' which concludes:—

> 'Mine was th' insensate frenzied part,
>   Ah! why should I such scenes outlive?
> Scenes so abhorrent to my heart!
>   'Tis thine to pity and forgive'—

which, but only after a considerable time, she did.

Still another lady is known to have been at the St. Cecilia concerts—another of that fair band of whom old George Thomson wrote: 'whose lovely faces at the concerts gave us the sweetest zest for music,'—Mrs. Richard A. Oswald of Auchencruive in Ayrshire, born Lucy Johnston of Hilton, East Lothian. It is said that Burns wrote in her honour the song whose chorus is—

> 'O, wat ye wha's in yon town,
>   Ye see the e'enin sun upon?
> The dearest maid's in yon town
>   That e'enin sun is shining on';

but 'thereby hangs a tale.'

Since 1792 Burns had been in correspondence with the now famous George Thomson, then the head clerk in the office of the Board of Manufactures in Edinburgh, who was devoting all his leisure to a life-work, the collecting, editing, and publishing of as complete a set as possible of the songs of Scotland set to music.

On 7th February 1795, Burns wrote to him from Ecclefechan thus:—'Do you know an air—I am sure you must know it—"We'll gang nae mair to yon toun"? I think in slowish time it would make an excellent song. I am highly delighted with it, and if you should think it worthy of your attention, I have a fair dame in my eye to whom I would consecrate it.

'Try it with this doggrel, till I give you a better:—

> '"O sweet to me yon spreading tree,
>   Where Jeanie wanders aft her lane,
> The hawthorn flower that shades her bower,
>   O when shall I behold again?"'

Burns, a little later, wrote a more elaborate version under the title, 'O, wat ye wha's in yon town,' in which 'Jeanie' again figures freely. This 'Jeanie' was probably Jean Lorimer, a farmer's daughter and the 'Chloris' and 'Lassie wi' the lint-white locks' of other songs. Desiring to compliment Mrs. Oswald of Auchencruive at the time she was residing at Dumfries, Burns merely changed the 'Jeanie' of this song to 'Lucy,' and, hey presto! 'twas done. If the 'Wandering Minstrel' in the *Mikado* had 'patriotic,' so with equal truth had Burns complimentary, 'ballads cut and dried.' C. K. Sharpe attributes the music of the song, 'O Mary! dear departed shade,' to Miss Johnston of Hilton, and adds that she gave double charms to a minuet and dignified a country dance. To this same lady was dedicated a collection of no less than sixty-eight new reels and strathspeys compiled and composed by Robert M'Intosh (1793).

We have very little doubt that another famous—we had almost said notorious—beauty of this time, Miss Burns (*alias* Matthews), would, during the course of the winter, put in an appearance at the concerts, for one of the few things we can gather about her is that 'she was always dressed in the latest fashion.' This lady, who had come to Edinburgh from Durham, caused quite a sensation about the time the poet Burns was in

Edinburgh, 'her youth [1] and beautiful figure' attracting notice wherever she went.

Now it happened that the windows of her rooms in Rose Street were overlooked by those of Lord Swinton's house, and in course of time her jealous neighbours 'began to talk,' and before many days were past Miss Burns found herself in the presence of no less a man than the well-known publisher, William Creech, at that time one of the magistrates of Edinburgh.

Creech, as the stern censor of his city's morals, sentenced the young lady to be banished furth of the city under penalty, if she returned, of six months' residence in the 'House of Correction.' Miss Burns's thoughts did not, however, naturally tend towards 'correction,' whether in the form of a house or otherwise, and so she entered an appeal in the Court of Session against this sentence, and not without effect, for—'tell it not in Gath'—the great Creech's judgment was overturned. Creech was literally furious: Edinburgh had not had for long so delightful a bit of scandal.

The newspapers now made fun freely at Creech's expense, publishing bogus announcements of marriage between the 'literary celebrity of Edinburgh' and 'Miss Burns of Rose Street in that City.' Miss Burns, in short, became the most talked-about person of the

[1] Twenty years.

hour. It is this Miss Burns who is the subject of Robert Burns's lines, 'Written underneath the picture of the celebrated Miss Burns':—

> 'Cease, ye prudes, your envious railing,
>   Lovely Burns has charms—confess;
> True it is, she had one failing,
>   Had a woman ever less?'

The poor girl appears to have been attacked not long after by that fatal malady euphemistically called 'the decline,' for she died in 1792 in the little village of Rosslyn, where she had gone for 'purer air': if all tales be true, she needed more than purer air to cure her. A stone in the churchyard of the little Pentland hamlet marks the spot where death claimed what was his of her who, after all, was only too human.

Continuing our list of patronesses of these famous old concerts, we may be safe in including Caroline Oliphant, the Baroness Nairne, for she was born in 1766 and died in 1845. About the heyday of these concerts, and at the time of Burns's visit, she would be just twenty-one; but it is in the highest degree probable that this gifted, poetical, aristocratic lady would, while in Edinburgh for the winter, attend one or two of the concerts in the Niddry Wynd—the only place at that time in the metropolis where the Scottish songs could be heard sung by the best professional voices of the day. It is inconceivable that the future authoress of 'The Auld Hoose,'

'The Rowan Tree,' 'Caller Herrin',' 'The Hundred Pipers,' 'The Laird o' Cockpen,' 'Will ye no come back again,' and 'The Land o' the Leal,' would not hear, if she possibly could, the finest renderings of the older songs of her native land, to whose already rich stores she was to add such treasures.

It amounts to a moral certainty that she who penned that exquisite mixture of humour, pathos, and satire in rattling rhyme, 'Caller Herrin',' must have listened below the venerable cupola of St. Cecilia's to the pathetic Scottish songs of the earlier epoch, for in Caroline Oliphant burned an intense love for Scotland, its scenery, its history, its dynasty—that same love which burned so brightly in Allan Ramsay, her father, not indeed according to the flesh, but after the inward law of the spirit of poetry.

We are not yet done with the belles who graced the Temple of the Muses in Niddry's Wynd, for there is still to be mentioned Miss Ferrier, a noted Edinburgh beauty. She was the eldest of the nine daughters of James Ferrier, W.S. (one of Scott's brethren at the table of the Clerks of Session), who lived for many years at 25 George Street, a few doors west of St. Andrew's Church. Susan Edmonston Ferrier, the authoress of *Marriage*, *Destiny*, and *Inheritance*, was a younger sister of the Miss Ferrier to whom Burns wrote the verses beginning—

> 'Nae heathen name shall I prefix
>   Frae Pindus or Parnassus;
> Auld Reekie dings them a' to sticks,
>   For rhyme-inspiring lasses.'

Burns had been, he tells us in the poem, going moodily along George Street in a sea-fog or 'haar,' when suddenly, on turning a corner, he nearly ran into Miss Ferrier, the fair sight of whom amid such gloom, both outside and inside, inspired him to write the verses commencing as above quoted, which conclude thus :—

> 'Ye turned a neuk—I saw your e'e—
>   She took the wing like fire!'

(alluding to his own melancholy). Miss Ferrier became the wife of General Graham of Stirling.

Continuing our list, we note another lady, a friend of Burns, a Miss Anne Stewart (daughter of John Stewart, Esq. of East Craig), who became the wife of an Edinburgh surgeon, Forrest Dewar. She is the Anna of two poems, in one of which occurs the verse :—

> 'Sweet Anna hath an air—a grace
>   Divine, majestic, touching;
> She talks, she charms, but who can trace
>   The process of bewitching?'

That Mrs. MacLehose—Burns's 'Clarinda'[1]—attended these concerts we have no direct evidence;

---

[1] Buried in the Canongate Churchyard.

but it is not at all unlikely that the vivacious and sentimental young widow—widow in effect, for her worthless husband had deserted her—would once or twice during the winter have procured a ticket for the concert, and taken a chair from the Potterrow, down the College Wynd, and along the Cowgate to the old hall, to bathe, as Holmes would put it, her poetical soul in the sea of sweet sounds created for her in that temple dedicated to St. Cecilia.

The afore-mentioned Miss Ferrier had a rival known as Miss Penzie M'Donald, whose baptismal name was Penelope, and whose father was Ronald M'Donald of Clanronald. Except in Miss Ferrier's eyes, this lady was acknowledged to be 'celebrated for the handsomeness of her figure and for her many accomplishments.' William Hamilton of Wishaw concurred so heartily in the prevailing opinion, that in March 1789 Miss Penzie became Mrs. Hamilton, and, ten years later, Lady Belhaven and Stenton, when the House of Lords had admitted her husband's claim to that then lapsed peerage.

Miss Isabella Macleod, of the famous family of Macleod of Raasay, must have been another patroness of the only concert in Edinburgh at the time Burns wrote the poem, 'On the Death of John Macleod, Esq., brother to a young lady a particular friend of the author.' Alluding to her bereavement and to the scenes 'beyond the tomb,' whither brother John had departed, Burns says:—

> 'Virtue's blossoms there shall blow
> And fear no withering blast;
> There Isabella's spotless worth
> Shall happy be at last.'

This lady was doomed to know much family sorrow. Her elder sister Flora, married only in 1779 to Col. Mure-Campbell of Rowallan, died in 1780 at the birth of her daughter. Miss Macleod's brother-in-law, the Earl of Loudon, shot himself; her father died at the comparatively early age of sixty-nine; and thus Burns, remembering all these her recent griefs, composed the song, 'Raving winds around her blowing'—a true lament in words set to a true lament in music.

The list of ladies may close with Miss Betsy Home, married to Captain Brown; Miss Cleghorn; Miss Jessie Chalmers, who became Mrs. Pringle of Haining, wife of Lord Haining; Miss Hay of Hayston, later Lady Forbes of Pitsligo; Miss Jardine, later Mrs. Home-Drummond of Blairdrummond; Miss Kinloch of Gilmerton, who married Sir Foster Cunliffe of Acton, Bart.; and Miss Halket of Pitferran, who became the wife of Count Lally-Tolendal.[1]

We must depart from our intention to make almost

[1] Chambers's *Traditions*, p. 275.

no mention of the male section of the audience in favour of two visitors, Sir Walter Scott and the Duc de Berri, whose fame and rank respectively may warrant their being admitted into the charmed circle of the 'dearer' sex.

We refuse for one moment to doubt that Walter Scott, as a young man in Edinburgh, attended during the winter season some of the concerts in St. Cecilia's Hall. Apart altogether from his own interest in music —as evinced by his having taken singing-lessons from Alexander Campbell of the Canongate, by his having been one of the directors of the Festival of 1815, and by his liking nothing better at Abbotsford than to listen to his daughters' playing — young Walter Scott moved in the best Edinburgh society, and the best Edinburgh society moved, one may say, in a body once a week to St. Cecilia's. In 1795 Walter Scott had already been acquainted with Miss Stuart of Belches for five years; and as all readers of Lockhart's *Life of Scott* will recollect, they both attended the Edinburgh assemblies.

Now we know for a certainty that the same 'set' that attended the assemblies attended the St. Cecilia concerts, for there are frequent announcements in the *Courant* that the hour of such-and-such a concert would be so-and-so, in order to allow 'ladies and gentlemen to attend the assembly afterwards.' What more likely than that young Scott would have ample opportunities for seeing, if not speaking to, Miss Stuart during those intervals in the concert when the audience were walking about in the area kept clear for that purpose?

Lord Balcarres, Walter Scott of Harden, a relative, and Sir William Forbes of Pitsligo, father of Scott's life-long friend, were all members of the Musical Society from 1790 onwards: as the guest of any of these families young Scott could have been in St. Cecilia's even had there been no lady-love as an additional attraction there at all. But possibly the strongest consideration of all to support this most interesting suggestion is the fact that Scott's father, Walter Scott, W.S., as his son himself tells us in that charming autobiography, actually played in the orchestra in St. Cecilia's. Scott says:—

'Robert was the only one of our family who could sing, though my father was musical, and a performer on the violoncello at the *gentlemen's concerts*' (1826). The italics are Scott's own. Can we dare to doubt that, even had young Walter no musical taste at all, he would, either from curiosity or because other members of the family were going to the concert, be certain to hear and to see his father in the *rôle* of 'celloist? But Alexander Campbell, his singing-master, never would allow that Walter Scott had a bad ear for music, and contended that if he did not understand music it was only because he did not choose to learn it. Once more, amongst the various friends of whom Scott in the autobiography gives us a list, there occurs one name with considerable musical interest attaching to it—'the Honourable Thomas Douglas, now Earl of Selkirk.' Scott is writing in 1808: it was the father, therefore, of Scott's friend—the Earl of Selkirk who entertained Burns—at whose house Urbani was a constant visitor, and used to get up little concerts with the daughters of the house.

The Earl of Selkirk who entertained Burns and Urbani was a member of the Musical Society, as may be seen by turning to Appendix III.

It is highly probable that his son, Scott's friend, on succeeding to the title would be elected to fill his father's place; at all events, one of Scott's most intimate acquaintances was a member of a musical family the head of which was a subscriber to the St. Cecilia concerts.

We have alluded to the fact that distinguished strangers were always welcomed at the concerts of the Musical Society.

Mr. Vogel must have been a proud man when he could send the following to the *Edinburgh Evening Courant* of March 29th, 1798 :—

'Under the patronage of His Royal Highness the

Duc de Berri,[1] who has given authority to say that he will honour the concert with his presence. Mr. Vogel takes the liberty of informing the nobility and others that his concert is fixed for Tuesday the 10th April in St. Cecilia's Hall.'

[1] The Duc de Berri, born 1778, died 1820, was the younger son of Charles X. of France, at this time an exile at Holyrood as the Comte d'Artois. In 1831 Charles X. returned to his old apartments at Holyrood, being accompanied by the Duchesse de Berri and her son Henri, Duc de Bordeaux.

CHAPTER VIII

THE RISE AND DEVELOPMENT OF THE CONCERT IN EDINBURGH

It is highly natural to look to the period immediately following the restoration of the Stuarts in order to find the first mention of such a thing as a concert in Edinburgh; nor are we surprised to discover that it is in the Palace of Holyrood, and there in the tennis-court by the Watergate, that both the drama and the concert of the Scottish metropolis may be said to have taken origin.

It is almost certain that, previously to the arrival of the Duke of York in 1679 as Commissioner from King Charles II. to his Scottish Parliament, theatrical representations had taken place under royal patronage in this same tennis-court of Holyrood.

James VI., in 1592, certainly permitted an English company of actors sent to Scotland by Queen Elizabeth to play here; and there are some who contend that on their visit in 1601, Shakespeare himself was a member of this company, which included his friend Burbage, and that therefore, in all probability,

Shakespeare acted along with him in this very place. There are descriptions in *Macbeth* explicable only on the supposition that Shakespeare did actually in his flesh see portions of Perthshire and Elgin. This company went to Perth, and some maintain it travelled even further north.

These were, of course, not by any means the first courtly revels that Holyrood had seen, for Queen Mary had got up a masked ball in which, to the everlasting scandalisation of her subjects, some of the ladies of the household had appeared in complete male costume. This, no doubt, was dramatic, but not 'legitimate drama.' The Duke and Duchess of York (Mary d'Este) and their daughter Anne (the Lady or Princess Anne, later Queen Anne) were in the habit of acting along with the household such pieces as Dryden's *Indian Emperor* and *The Spanish Friar* in the tennis-court, no doubt in presence of the nobility and gentry who at that time constituted the society of Edinburgh and Canongate.

Dryden himself notices the emigration to Edinburgh of certain lights in the literary and artistic world when he says :—

'Our brethren have from Thames to Tweed departed,
To Edinburgh gone, or washed or carted.'[1]

---

[1] Prologue to the University of Oxford, No. xxxvii. of *Prologues and Epilogues*.

In addition to plays, concerts seem to have been given, if not in the tennis-court, then under the direct patronage of the ducal 'set.' But the earliest distinct mention in Old Edinburgh records of a concert of music seems to be one quoted by Chambers in his *Domestic Annals of Scotland*:—'A man named Beck, with some associates, had now (1694) erected a concert of music.'

The fact that in the following year, 1695, there was given at Holyrood on St. Cecilia's Day, November 22nd, a fairly ambitious instrumental concert, with more amateurs than professionals in it, proves to us that music had had others than Beck to woo it with notable success.

Of this festival concert we have two accounts—the earliest from the pen of William Tytler of Woodhouselee, who wrote in 1792,[1] and a much later one by Robert Chambers in his *Domestic Annals*.[2]

Tytler calls his paper, 'On the fashionable amusements and entertainments in Edinburgh in the last century, with a plan of a grand concert of music on St. Cecilia's Day, 1695.'

Although the author had certainly not been present, he had, writing in 1792, sources of information for ever lost to us now, in which connection it may be mentioned

[1] *Transactions of the Society of Antiquaries of Scotland*, vol. i., 1792.   [2] Vol. iii.

Rise of the Concert in Edinburgh 251

that he knew Andrew Dickson, the Duke of York's golf-caddie on Leith Links.

The article, a gossipy and readable one, begins by saying that a hundred years before, 1690, there was a great taste for music in the Scottish metropolis, and contrasts that condition with the 'present languid spirit of music.' The orchestra was made up of over thirty performers, nineteen of whom were gentlemen of the 'first rank and fashion,' while the eleven professionals were 'masters of music.' The players were divided thus: of first violins, seven; of second violins, five; of flutes, six; of hautbois, two; of violoncellos and viol-da-gambas, five; and there was one harpsichord. The pieces played were chiefly *motetti* of Bassani and the sonatas of Corelli.

Amongst the amateurs were Lord Colville of Ochiltree, Lord Elcho, Mr. John Middleton (afterwards General Middleton), Sir John Pringle, Mr. Seton of Pitmedden, Mr. Falconer of Phesdo, Mr. Carse, Keeper of Parliamentary Records, and a Mr. W. Thomson. These gentlemen are described as skilled in music, and good players on the violin, harpsichord, flute, and hautbois.

The concert was arranged and conducted by Henry Crumbden, a German, 'long,' says Chambers, 'the Orpheus in the musical school of Edinburgh.'

Amongst the gentlemen, Christie of Newhall played the viol-da-gamba, Seton of Pitmedden one of the first violins. Robert, Lord Colville of Ochiltree, a great musical enthusiast, is reported to have 'understood counterpoint well.' His instruments were the harpsichord and organ, and while in Italy he had gathered together a very large collection of music. Defoe in his poem *Caledonia*, Part III., thus alludes to him :—

> 'The God of Musick joyns when Colville plays,
> And all the Muses dance to Haddington's essays.'

He died unmarried in 1728, having been a peer for fifty-seven years.

Sir Gilbert Elliot of Minto, another Scottish amateur, was the first to introduce the German flute into Scotland.

Amongst the professionals was Daniel Thomson, one of the king's trumpeters, father of William Thomson, a boy at the time of the concert in 1695. William Thomson in 1725 published in London the first collection of Scots songs *set to music*, the appearance of which is believed to have created the English rage for Scottish music which did undoubtedly exist from this date onward. The volume is entitled, '*Orpheus Caledonius*, or, A Collection of the best Scotch Songs set to musick by W. Thomson, London : engraved and printed for the author at his house in Leicester Fields. . . . Folio.' It contains fifty songs, and is dedicated to the Princess of Wales, afterwards Queen Caroline;

seven of the tunes are attributed to Rizzio, but in the second (1733) edition this is omitted. William Thomson had a very fine voice, and was often invited to the Court to sing Scots songs there.

Through the courtesy of the Queen's and Lord Treasurer's Remembrancer, search in the records of the Exchequer Office at Edinburgh has discovered that 'Daniel Thomson, musician in Edinburgh,' received his commission as State Trumpeter dated 28th February 1705-1706.

To give any account, however fragmentary, of the history of musical literature in Scotland is outside the scope of this work, but we may notice the works produced by other two musicians who played in that long-forgotten St. Cecilia Festival concert.

Of Adam Craig, Mr. Tytler says he 'was reckoned a good orchestra player on the violin and teacher of music. I remember him as the second violin to M'Gibbon in the Gentlemen's Concert.' (This was the concert in Steil's tavern and in Mary's Chapel.)

In 1730, Adam Craig published at Edinburgh '*A Collection of the Choicest Scots Tunes*, adapted for the Harp or Spinnet, and within the compass of the Voice, Violin, or German Flute, by Adam Craig, Edinburgh, 1730. R. Cooper, *fecit*. Entered in Stationers' Hall.' (Oblong, folio.)

It is dedicated 'To the Honourable Lords and

Gentlemen of the Musical Society of Mary's Chappell,' as the 'generous encouragers and promoters of music.' Craig died at the Boroughmuirhead, near Edinburgh, in September 1741, and was buried in Greyfriars' Churchyard, the following being a copy of the entry of his interment from the books of the records, kindly extracted by Mr. J. G. Ferguson, Keeper of the Records:—

'Sep. 3rd, 1741.
Adam Craig. Musician.
4. D. P. E. ye corner Foulis Tomb'

William M'Gibbon, the son of a performer in this concert, Matthew M'Gibbon, was a violinist and composer born about the beginning of the eighteenth century. Between 1740 and 1755, M'Gibbon issued three books of collections of Scottish tunes, as well as a set of sonatas or solos for a German flute or violin. M'Gibbon, who had studied the violin under Corbet in London, was leader of the Gentlemen's Concerts in Edinburgh. William M'Gibbon also wrote dances and flute music. Robert Fergusson has a poem which makes reference to the death of William M'Gibbon. The following is the entry of interment from the Greyfriars' records:—

'1756. October 5th.
Mr. William M'Gibbon. Musician.
4. D. P. E. Drummond's Tomb.'

Rise of the Concert in Edinburgh

For a complete history of Scottish musical literature consult Stenhouse, *Lyric Poetry and Music of Scotland*.[1]

We are still in point of date in 1695, nor do we find any mention of music till at the end of the second decade of the following century, if we except the mention of a concert in the tennis-court arranged by a Mr. Abel in 1705 under the patronage of the Duke of Argyll. In 1718, of those who played in 1695 there were still alive and in Edinburgh only Adam Craig, second violin at the Gentlemen's Concerts, and William M'Gibbon, now leader and first violin, reported as playing Corelli, Geminiani, and Handel with great skill.

In the *Edinburgh Courant* for July 12th, 1720, we find a quaint paragraph to the effect that Mr. Gordon, who had lately been travelling in Italy for his improvement in music, was daily expected in Edinburgh, accompanied by Signor Lorenzo Bocchi, who is considered the second master of the violoncello in Europe and the fittest hand to join Mr. Gordon's voice in the 'consorts' with which he designs to entertain his friends before 'the rising of the session.'

This Mr. Gordon evidently remained in Edinburgh after his arrival with Bocchi, for we are told that in May 1722 he was invited by several Glasgow gentlemen to give a 'consort' in that city.

[1] Blackwood, 1853.

This he did, and immediately afterwards he published 'Proposals for the improvement of music in Scotland, together with a most reasonable and easy scheme for establishing a pastoral opera in Edinburgh.'

Without doubt the period from 1695 to about 1725 is, relatively speaking, destitute of musical incident. But the reason is not far to seek: the times were socially very unsettled: in comparatively few years a series of changes effected not without much heart-burning had swept over Edinburgh, giving her citizens much graver things to think of than plays or concerts.

The affable Duke of York—for he had always treated the Scottish nobility with courteous consideration—had left Holyrood to assume the crown left him by his gay brother; and thus by 1685, James, Duke of York, was James the Seventh and Second—papist and bigot.

By 1688 the Revolution had occurred, and William and Mary ascended the throne of Great Britain: by 1702 Queen Anne had begun to reign.

The years that closed the seventeenth and ushered in the eighteenth century were years full of too much political fermentation to afford the necessary tranquillity for the growth of any very generally shared artistic life in the Scottish capital.

For many were the sources of unrest abroad: there were the Jacobites just rising into existence, ready to recall the abdicated James; the Whigs staunch in their

Rise of the Concert in Edinburgh

support of the Protestant Succession—was it not the collision of these parties that stained the Garry blood-red at Killiecrankie?—there were very numerous religious disturbances, protests and persecutions, that made the martyr's cry as common as the peewit's upon the moors of Scotland, that kept up a constant supply of heads for the Tolbooth and the Nether Bow Port; and there had just occurred the Union, than which no political proposal had ever before so shaken the whole nation to its deepest depths with a more genuine alarm,—little wonder then that music did verily languish in the old metropolis.

For at this time, whatever happened either in London or in Scotland's remotest glen at once affected her capital. Four monarchs within twenty years—that could not but affect her somewhat; the Scottish Privy Council in that grim old subterranean chamber—with cultured Rosehaugh, scheming Queensberry, and wily old Tarbat—taking cognisance of every psalm sung by every old Cameronian in the wilds of Galloway,— all these things kept Edinburgh, the seat of Government, of Law, of Ecclesiastical Congress, in a state of constant commotion.

By 1710 or so, things had quieted down somewhat: the Edinburgh of Queen Anne was beginning to establish its reputation for learning, legal lore, culture, wit, and conviviality; and hence, with a return to more tranquil conditions, we find the sweet science of music claiming her own. It was not to be expected that her harmonies could co-exist with the discords of political and ecclesiastical strife.

About this time a number of gentlemen, musical amateurs, had been in the habit of assembling in the long evenings of the northern winter to practise pieces on their violins in one of the taverns patronised by the majority of their 'set.' For Edinburgh has always been dominated by 'sets'—legal, ecclesiastical, medical, professorial, artistic, and so on; and each had its own 'seat of election' in a tavern, or club-house, as we would now call its modern representative.

Their name is legion, these out-of-the-way, almost subterranean, dimly lighted taverns—one noted for its particular kind of ale, another for its good-looking landlady, another for the eccentricity of its host, another for its oysters and porter, another because on such-and-such a day in each week, such-and-such a club would get drunk in it.

The names of some of them are of the web and woof of Old Edinburgh story: Dawnie Douglas's, headquarters of the 'Crochallan Fencibles'; Johnnie Dowie's of Liberton's Wynd, called the 'Coffin,' and a 'howff' successively of Fergusson and Burns; Lucky Fykie's 'o' the Patter-ra''; the 'Star and Garter,' kept by Cleriheugh in Writer's Court—the

Rise of the Concert in Edinburgh

Cleriheugh's of *Guy Mannering*, and the scene of Councillor Pleydell's 'high jinks'; Steil's or the 'Cross Keys'; Fortune's, and a score of others. The mention of a tavern called the 'Cross Keys' brings us to the establishment in 1725 of the first musical society in Scotland, with the title, naturally enough, of 'The Musical Society of Edinburgh.'

Now, there were in Old Edinburgh two taverns with the sign of the 'Cross Keys,' one Fortune's tavern in Old Stamp Office Close, the other Steil's or Steel's in the Old Assembly Close, as we now call it, or Steil's Close, as it was then called.

We have no great difficulty in deciding in which of these two houses of entertainment the old amateur orchestral society used to meet, because the house known about 1760 to 1770 as 'Fortune's tavern of the Cross Keys' was at the earlier epoch (1725) the town residence of the Earls of Eglinton.

On the other hand we have, relatively speaking, not a little direct evidence as to the other 'Cross Keys,' kept by one Patrick or 'Pate' Steil, who was not only a performer on the violin, but maker of that instrument and a judge of musical instruments in general. His tavern (the original fabric of it) perished in a great fire in 1708, but of course the close was rebuilt: it was therefore the old tavern of Steil's that Dr. Archibald Pitcairne, who died in 1713, praises in his

Latin poems upon the houses of public entertainment in the Edinburgh of his day. 'At one time,' he says, 'you may be delighted with the bowls of Steil of the Cross Keys.' Pitcairne was a poet, and presumably artistic and a Bohemian; he therefore would find congenial company at a place where the landlord, who was musical, had guests who were also amateur musicians. Dr. Pitcairne, a fervent admirer of the ladies, could meet them here, for it is recorded that ladies were guests at the concert in Steil's tavern, since 'it was a point of re-union for the *beau monde* of Edinburgh in days while as yet there were neither theatres nor balls.'[1]

More, however, is known as to Patrick Steil himself. John Reid in his *New Lights on Old Edinburgh*—a book which does not belie its title so far as our present topic is concerned—assures us that from title-deeds to Old Edinburgh properties, 'Robert Mylne of Balfargie' and 'Patrick Steil, Merchant Burgess,' were about the year 1681 heritable proprietors of certain houses west of Writer's Court. In other words, Steil was not a nobody in Queen Anne's Edinburgh.

It would be strange if Allan Ramsay, a poet and a convivial man, had not something to say of this Steil's. He does indeed mention a Steil's as a tavern that he knew, but he leaves us no clear idea as to which close or wynd it was hidden in; yet as the name cannot

[1] Chambers's *Domestic Annals of Scotland.*

have been common, we are probably not far wrong in thinking that Ramsay too has written of Pate's.

But Patrick Steil was more than a landlord and a musician: he was in 1681 one of the captains in the 'Trained Bands' of Edinburgh. It is recorded that he had assigned to his care 'The west side of Warriston's Close and ending with Archibald Douglas on the west side of the Old Provost's' (Fleshmarket Close).

Further, on one occasion during Steil's captaincy, the trained bands met in the tavern in question in Steil's Close. This had been previously known as 'Durie's Close,' from its having contained the mansion of Sir Alexander Gibson of Durie, Lord Durie, whose house stood on the site on which the Assembly Rooms were afterwards erected.

At a still earlier date, in the middle of the sixteenth century, this same close had been known as 'Little's Close,' from Clement Little, brother of the well-known provost of that name. Perhaps the most recent mention of this tavern under the up-to-date spelling 'Steel's' is in Omond's life of *Fletcher of Saltoun* [1] The author conjectures that the Scottish patriot may have been arrested in this tavern on the eve of his duel with the Earl of Roxburgh. Fletcher of Saltoun was a great friend of Pitcairne; and as Pitcairne was an *habitué*

[1] P. 122. (Famous Scots Series. Oliphant, Anderson, and Ferrier, Edinburgh. March 1897.)

of Steil's tavern, it is most likely that they met in this place—no great distance from the Parliament Hall, whence Fletcher had just come to take rest after passing through one of its stormiest Union debates.

But finally, Chambers has no doubt whatever as to Steil's being a tavern frequented by politicians, and the scene of the founding of the Musical Society of Edinburgh, for, writing of the exciting days just before the Union was consummated, he says:[1]—

'Politicians met in taverns to discuss the affairs of State. One situated in the High Street, kept by Patrick Steil, was the resort of a number of patriots who urged on the "Act of Security" and resisted the Union, and the phrase "Pate Steil's Parliament" occasionally appears in the correspondence of the time. It was in the same place that the weekly concert was commenced.'

This was in 1725: to whom then does the following announcement in the *Caledonian Mercury* of February 1729 have reference?—'A sale by auction of the haill pictures, prints, music-books, and musical instruments belonging to Mr. *John* Steil.' Very probably to a son or other relative of Patrick, who had, we may suppose, assumed the business on the death or retirement of Steil the elder. The mention of the music is too significant to allow us to imagine that it was the property of any other family of Steil.

[1] *Domestic Annals of Scotland.*

Signor BOCCHI had been in Edinburgh for some years previously to 1726, and not idle either, for we read in the *Caledonian Mercury* of February 22nd, 1726, that 'Signor Lorenzo Bocchi has published an opera of his own composition by subscription, containing twelve sonatas or solos for different instruments, viz. a violin, flute, violoncello, viol-de-gamba, and Scots cantate with instrumental parts after the Italian manner, the words by Mr. Ramsay, with a Thorow Bass for the Harpsichord. Subscribers may have their copies *at Mr. John Steill's* any time before the first of March ensuing.' This is the same work that figures in Allan Ramsay's poems as 'A Scots Cantata, music by L. Bocchi.' The *Caledonian Mercury*, June 1729, mentions a concert of Bocchi's in the 'Taylors' Hall,' Cowgate.[1]

By 1728 the Society had become sufficiently established to give weekly performances of vocal and instrumental music.

They were henceforth to be known as the 'Gentlemen's Concerts,' but, as we have seen, ladies were frequently guests. At this time the society numbered about seventy persons, not indeed all of them amateur, for they had engaged such professionals as could be procured to assist them in rendering on violin and harpsichord the

[1] Dr. Burney mentions a singer, Boschi, for whom Handel wrote some of his finest bass songs.

sonatas of Corelli, and the just-published concertos and overtures of Handel.

But by this time the Society had evidently found their old quarters in Steil's tavern too confined, for in this year they moved to a place better suited to their purpose—St. Mary's Chapel in the Niddry Wynd. In the first two chapters we mentioned this old place, long ago demolished; but it is to the concert *here* that Ramsay alludes in the lines on the fly-leaf of this book :—

> 'Our concert now nae mair the ladies mind,
> They 've a' forgot the gait to Niddery's Wynd';

and it is this St. Mary's Chapel that he describes when he writes of Oswald :—

> 'No more thy solemn bass's awful sound
> Shall from *the Chapel's vaulted roof* rebound.'

From the account by Maitland which we give in Chapter VI., it appears that in 1728 the Musical Society or Club was re-organised and its membership extended. Here then, from 1728 to 1762, did all that was brightest and best in Scottish music flourish in peace; here it was that the newly-published oratorios of Handel were performed for the first time in Scotland. Thus Adam Craig in 1730 dedicates his *Collection of Scots Tunes for the Spinet* to the lords and gentlemen of the Musical Society of *St. Mary's Chappell*. It is to

Rise of the Concert in Edinburgh

this period of the existence of the Musical Society—the St. Mary's Chapel period—that the musical publications of Maclean, Oswald, M'Gibbon, Barsanti, and Bremner belong.

Maclean's is 'dedicated to the Honourable the Governor and Members of the Musical Society.' Oswald's collections were published by him after he left Edinburgh for London, which move was the cause of Ramsay's lament for him, a portion of which we have already quoted.[1]

The St. Mary's Chapel period of the Edinburgh concerts is by no means destitute of professional musicians, both British and foreign, who sojourned here for a time and left their names in the city's annals.

Two of them, Lampe and Pasquali, entered Edinburgh to visit it, but they died there and were buried within its gates.

JOHANN FRIEDRICH LAMPE was born in the year 1703 at Helmstadt in Saxony, and died at Edinburgh on July 25th, 1751. In 1725, on coming to England, he was engaged as 'bassoon-player at the Opera,' where Handel's then quite new operas were being given.

In London he married Isabella Young, sister of Mrs. Thomas Augustine Arne, and daughter of Charles Young, organist of All Hallows', Barking, London. A burlesque opera, entitled *The Dragon of Wantley*,

[1] Chapter VI. p. 192.

which he composed about this time to words of Carey's, was a distinct success.

The *Edinburgh Evening Courant* of February 21st, 1751, announced that there was to be performed, a day or two later, 'at the benefit of Mr. Storer, in the Concert Hall in the Canongate, a burlesque opera called *The Dragon of Wantley*. The Musick composed by Mr. Lamp.'

Lampe, accompanied by his wife, arrived in Edinburgh in 1750 on their way from Dublin, whither they had gone in 1748.

Lampe attempted to introduce in Edinburgh open-air concerts, which doubtless were as common in his day in the 'Fatherland' as in ours, but from his very announcement it would seem that he had misgivings as to the success of the *al fresco* under our grey sky. His advertisement in the *Edinburgh Evening Courant* of June 3rd, 1757, is :—' Mr. Lampe proposes to hold his first concert to-morrow, the 4th June, in Heriot's Gardens at 6 in the evening, in case the weather is not unfavourable.'

But Mrs. Lampe was not silent, as the following announcement from the same newspaper testifies, March 12th, 1751 :—'For the benefit of Mr. Lampe, at the Concert Hall in the Cowgate on Wednesday 13th, will be performed a concert of music, after the first part of the concert, Shakespeare's *King John*.

To which will be added (gratis) the opera of operas called *Tom Thumb the Great*. The music performed by Mr. Lampe; the part of Tom Thumb to be performed by Mrs. Lampe. To begin at 6 P.M.'

On 26th March 1751, Lampe conducted in the same place a performance of *Acis and Galatea,* in which Mrs. Lampe took one of the vocal parts.

Lampe published a good deal one way and another. Besides composing many single songs which he collected in the *Lyra Britannica*, he published in 1737 '*A plain, compendious method of teaching Thorough Bass after the most rational manner,* with proper rules for practice.'

Lampe died in Edinburgh on 25th July 1751, and was buried in the Canongate Churchyard on the 28th.

The following is extracted from the Canongate register of burials in the Register House:—

'Lamp. July 28th, 1751.
'John Frederick Lamp, Music Master, in his own and Butcher's B(urial) p(lace). Fever. 48.'

It would be hard to beat this for official brevity.

By the side of this grave a tall mural tombstone was erected; but as it faces the west, the lettering is, after nearly a century and a half, very difficult to decipher.

Surmounting the stone are two angels, now not only wingless, but with their once plump limbs fractured, who face each other and hold between them an open book, on the left page of which is written 'John Frederick Lampe,' on the right some bars of music. The inscription runs thus:—

> 'Here lye the mortal remains of John Frederick Lampe, whose harmonious compositions shall outlive all monumental register, and with melodious notes through future ages perpetuate his fame till time shall sink into eternity.[1]
> 'His taste for moral harmony appears throughout all his conduct. He was a most loving husband, affectionate father, trusty companion . . .'

but what else he was is entirely wiped from the stone by 'Time's effacing fingers.' Brown's *Dictionary of Musicians* (1883), however, continues it thus:—

> 'On the 23rd[2] of July, in the forty-eighth year of his age, he was summoned to join that heavenly concert with the blessed choir above, where his virtuous soul now enjoys that harmony which was his chief delight upon earth. *In vita felicitate dignos mors reddit felices.*'

In 1751 two harpsichords of Lampe's were advertised for sale.

NICOLA PASQUALI or PASQUALE, and his wife Signora PASQUALE, were Italians, who figure somewhat conspicuously in the pre-Saint Cecilian Hall days. Signor

---

[1] The rest is not legible. It is extracted from Mackay's *Burgh of the Canongate*, 1879.   [2] 25th?

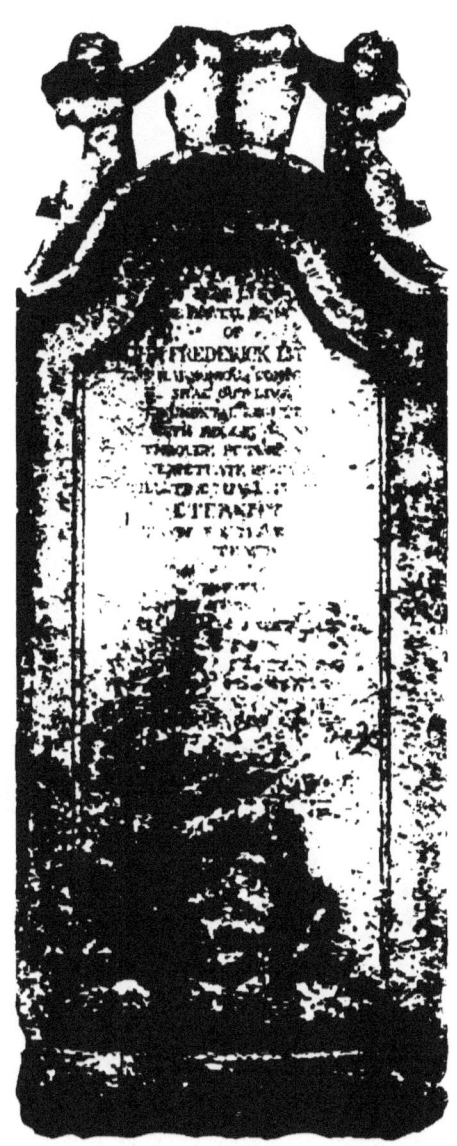

TOMB OF JOHN FREDERICK LAMPE, IN THE
CANONGATE CHURCHYARD, EDINBURGH.

Pasquale seems to have been born about 1718, and to have first appeared in London in 1743. In Edinburgh he was engaged as 'professional musician for the Gentlemen's Concerts.' The *Edinburgh Evening Courant* of 9th October 1752 announces, 'at Assembly Hall tomorrow, a grand concert of vocal and instrumental music. Mr. Storer to take a vocal part; violin, Signor Pasquale, and Signor Pasquale, junior, on the violoncello, "being the first time of their performing in this kingdom."'

The Pasquales were lodging in November 1752 at 'Mr. Coustin's in Shoemakers' Land, facing the Earl of Murray's in the Canongate.' Signor Pasquale conducted a benefit concert for Mr. Storer at the Taylors' Hall, Cowgate, in December 1752.

While resident these five years in Edinburgh, Pasquale and his brother taught singing as well as the harpsichord, and they announced[1] that they would instruct 'gratis any poor girl with an extraordinary good strong voice.'

Pasquale composed twelve overtures for full band, music for two violins, as well as songs, and was the author of a treatise on the *Art of fingering the Harpsichord*.

We insert part of a programme of a benefit concert for Signor Pasquale :—'On January 17th, for the Benefit

[1] *Edinburgh Evening Courant*, Nov. 27th, 1752.

of Signor Pasquali, a concert of vocal and instrumental music, the vocal part by Miss Rodburne, the instrumental by Signor Pasquali and others.

PART I.

Overture in *Pharamond* by Mr. Handel.
Song, "Caro mio ben perdona," by Signor Lampugnani.
Concerto on the German Flute, performed by Mr. M'Pherson.
Song, "When Charming Beauty," in *Noalis*, by Signor Pasquali.
La Chasse, a new solo for the violin.

PART II.

Full piece with Trumpets, French Horns, Kettledrums.
Song, "Tortido in volto"—a capital song—by Signor Pergolesi.'

Pasquale died at Edinburgh on the 13th, and was buried on the 15th October 1757, in the Canongate Churchyard. The entry runs:—'Nicolla Pasquali, musician. South from Bishop Keeth's B. P. Fluxes. 39.' There is no stone to mark the spot—in all probability none was erected over the stranger's grave.

Contemporaneous with the Pasquales were Signor and Signora PASSERINI, who were engaged by the Musical Society of Edinburgh, *i.e.* the Gentlemen's

Rise of the Concert in Edinburgh

Concert of Mary's Chapel, which engagement, they announce in the *Edinburgh Evening Courant* of August 1872, 'will end with the current year.' They had arrived before 1751, and in July of that year were lodging in rooms at the 'first turnpike below Blackfriars' Wynd.'

Passerini in 1752 advertises [1] that he teaches singing, violin, and 'Thorow Bass' on the harpsichord, and he and the Signora announce the same year that they are about to institute 'concerts after the manner of oratorios.' A month or two later Mons. and Madame Passerini advertise a 'spiritual concert after the manner of oratorios,' these to be held twice every month. Passerini describes himself as 'concert-master of the Musical Society at Edinburgh.'

On 8th August 1752 they had a benefit concert in Mary's Chapel, in which Passerini played a 'solo on the violin or viole d'amour.' [2] Signora Passerini and

---

[1] *Edinburgh Evening Courant.*

[2] The following may be taken as a typical programme; we give it in full:—

On Tuesday the 18th of August, for the benefit of Signor and Signora Passerini, at Mary's Chapel in Niddry's Wynd, beginning at 5 o'clock.

    I. Act.—Overture by Mr. Handel in occasional oratorios.
        Signora Passerini's English song, 'Ye men of Gaza,' in *Samson*.
        Solo upon the violin or viole d'amour by Mr. Passerini.

a Signor Rochetti frequently sang duets at concerts about this time—more than once at Mr. M'Pherson's concert in the Assembly Hall.

'Madam Passerini' had a benefit concert of her own on 16th July 1751 in the Assembly Hall, on which occasion she sang 'a duetta with Mr. Rochetti.'

On December 25th, 1752,[1] there is a quaint announcement by the Passerinis that on the 26th inst. their sixth concert after the manner of oratorios will take place at 6 P.M. (tickets 2s. 6d.), and 'the remaining three concerts will be still better than any which Signor and Signora Passerini have performed here.'

The other musicians of this period, who have left little trace save their names in the newspaper announce-

>Mrs. Passerini's English song, 'Total Eclipse,' in *Samson*.
>II. Act.—Miss Meyer's English song, 'To make mankind,' by Mr. Morgan.
>Solo upon the violin or viole d'amour by Mr. Passerini.
>Mrs. Passerini's the fine cantata of Signor Pergolesi, never produced in Edinburgh, 'Luce degli occhi miei.'
>III. Act.—Mrs. Passerini's Scots song, 'Tweedside.'
>Sinfonia by Signor Passerini.
>New duetto by Signor Araya, 'A si te fui crudele.'
>Tickets three shillings.

[1] *Edinburgh Evening Courant.*

Rise of the Concert in Edinburgh 275

ments of concerts, may be comprised in the following list :—

1. Mr. Berry.
2. Mr. Davis.
3. Madame de Frenc.
4. H. de Monti (author of *The Self-Taught Musician: a Treatise on Music*).
5. Mr. Gordon.
6. Mr. M'Glashan (in 1770 in Berranger's Close; in 1779 at foot of Skinner's Close).
7. Mr. M'Pherson (living in 1768 in Bell's Wynd).
8. Miss Meyer.
9. Signor Lampugnani.
10. Signor Pescatore.
11. Mr. Philips.
12. Miss Rodburne.
13. Signor Rochetti.
14. Mr. Rock.
15. Mr. Christian Rich.
16. Mr. and Mrs. Storer (in 1752 in Miln's Land, Canongate).
17. Mr. Thomson.

During this pre-Saint Cecilian period we see then that besides in St. Mary's Chapel, concerts were held in—

1. The Taylors' Hall, Cowgate.
2. The Assembly Rooms, Assembly Close.

3. The Concert Hall, or the New Concert Hall (Canongate Theatre, Playhouse Close).

The weekly gentlemen's concert was not regularly advertised, but only when it was decided to admit ladies as guests of the members. Thus, to take an example:—

Edinburgh Evening Courant, July 17th, 1749.—'The Gentlemen of the Musical Society have appointed a concert for ladies at Mary's Chapel on Friday next, the 21st inst., at 5 o'clock afternoon. The members will please call for their tickets on Wednesday and Thursday next, at Mr. James Carmichael's writing-chamber in James Court, west entry and fifth door downstairs. No more than sixty tickets are to be given out, and no ladies to be admitted without tickets.'

The following announcement, dated January 16th, 1755, must have been Amen-ed by more than one male voice:—

'We hear that on Tuesday last Signor Pasquali had a general rehersal of the music that is to be performed at the *Assembly Hall* for his Benefit, and as it is expected that the company will be numerous, many ladies have resolved to go *without hoops*, as they did at the last St. Cecilia's Concert.'

In 1749 the fee for membership of the Musical Society was one guinea; in 1752 it had risen to one and a half guineas; by 1778 it had risen to two guineas.

In 1762 the Musical Society of Edinburgh moved into its still larger premises in St. Cecilia's Hall in the same wynd, and remained in that habitation and with that name until 1801, when it met for the last time (February 17th) in the old hall to dispose of its property. No concert had indeed been given in it since the spring of 1798. Care must be taken in reading Old Edinburgh records to distinguish between St. Cecilia's Concert Hall, the only concert-hall of Edinburgh, and what was variously and mysteriously called 'The Concert Hall in the Canongate,' or 'The New Concert Hall,' as well as from 'The Concert Hall in the Cowgate,' or 'The Concert in the Taylors' Hall.'

To explain fully what the Canongate or Cowgate 'Concert' was, would be to enter into the history of the theatrical stage in Edinburgh—a subject outside the limits of this work; but briefly, these expressions may be said to have been used as 'blinds' or 'decoys.' The theatre in Playhouse Close, Canongate, had been built about 1746 as the first licensed theatre in Scotland, previously to which theatrical companies had acted in the Taylors' Hall in the Cowgate—a building in no way adapted for such a purpose.

But this was not the first theatrical venture in Edinburgh: every one knows how Allan Ramsay in 1736 had ruined himself financially (and the Town Council and clergy thought morally as well) by refitting at his own expense a building in Carrubber's Close, known as The Theatre.

The feeling on the part of the Town Council against

'stage-plays' was at this time so strong that the manager of the company either in the Taylors' Hall or later in the Canongate Theatre would advertise 'a concert of music' on such-and-such a night. Every one knew that a play was going to be acted; occasionally some purely musical performance was given before the play began, oftener not. In this way the edict of the Town Council forbidding plays was technically evaded, but that acting went on was an open secret. This peculiarity, however, requires to be borne in mind, else such an expression as 'the company belonging to the concert in Taylors' Hall' seems quite unintelligible, when one knows there was, properly speaking, only one concert-hall in the old city. This feeling on the part of the clergy extended, it would appear, to musical as well as to theatrical performances, for after the great fire of November 1824 one of the ministers of the city preached a sermon on 'The importance of hearing the voice of God,' in which he attributed the calamity to the Musical Festival of the previous 25th October. Many people seriously thought that the fire was a judgment from Heaven on account of so-called 'sacred' music having been performed at the Festival.

By the end of 1798 we can already hear the swan-song of the dying Society. On December 22nd, 1798, the *Edinburgh Evening Courant* published the following: —'The Governor and Directors of the Musical Society hereby give notice that a general meeting of the Society is to be held in St. Cecilia's Hall on Monday, 24th December current, at 2 P.M. . . . for the purpose of finally determining whether the Society shall be immediately dissolved or continued on the present or any other plan.'

So our old friend the 'Musical Society of Edinburgh' came to an end by a decorous *auto da fé* after a continuous existence of seventy-five years. From 1800 until 1815 we find few allusions to public music in Edinburgh.

Stark's *Picture of Edinburgh* was published during this very period (1806), and it is therefore interesting to have the views of a contemporary writer upon things musical:[1]—

'Perhaps at no period in the annals of Scottish music was this art more universally cultivated than at present. It forms a general part of modern education, and few are to be met with who cannot sing or play upon one instrument or another. The decline is only in the public exhibitions, and the want of proper encouragement to these proceeds more perhaps from the manner in which they are conducted and the pieces which are there performed, than from any want of taste in the inhabitants of Edinburgh. . . .

'Since the weekly concerts in St. Cecilia's Hall were

[1] Page 375.

given up, subscription concerts have been performed in the Assembly Rooms, George Street, and at Corri's Rooms (formerly Royal Circus). In one season no less than two musical exhibitions were encouraged in Edinburgh. But this was chiefly owing to a competition, and the result did not prove much to the satisfaction of the rivals, although performers of the first merit were engaged on both sides. One of these, under the direction of Mr. Urbani, a well-known vocal performer, was held in the Assembly Rooms, and the other under the superintendence of Mr. N. Corri, in the buildings of the late amphitheatre. The former of these was obliged to be given up; and the annual concerts during the winter are now performed solely at Corri's Rooms.

'For the last two years the annual concerts have been well conducted, and met with very considerable patronage. Mr. Corri, with an attention to the public highly meritorious, has spared no efforts in procuring excellent performers, and the concerts during that period have perhaps never been exceeded for variety in Edinburgh.'

Stark specially mentions 'Fischer, Salomon, Jarnowick, and Cramer' as being the chief lights at St. Cecilia's in its later years.

In 1790 the professional musicians in Edinburgh formed themselves into 'The Edinburgh Musical Fund,' which was a society to provide relief for their widows and orphans: for several years thereafter it gave an annual concert in St. Cecilia's.

A letter in the *Evening Courant* of March 6th, 1809, does indeed appear, urging the revival of the St. Cecilia concerts, but it called forth no action. The nation was passing through deep waters at this time in connection with our expensive Continental wars, and all departments of æsthetic culture suffered a blight from which some of them have recovered only within the last few years.

In 1815, however, a prolonged musical festival was carried out, an account of which may be read in a little book by George Farquhar Graham, entitled '*The First Edinburgh Musical Festival*, held between October 30th and November 5th.'[1]

The following gentlemen, amongst others, acted as directors — Mr. (later Sir) Walter Scott, Henry M'Kenzie ('The Man of Feeling'),[2] Sir William Fettes, the Hon. Henry Erskine, Principal Baird, Gilbert Innes of Stow,[2] and Lord Grey.

The morning performances were to take place in Parliament Hall, while Corri's Rooms were considered more suitable for the evening ones. Six transferable tickets cost £3, 3s.

On the first morning (31st October) the overture to

[1] James Ballantyne and Co., 1816.
[2] Buried in Greyfriars'.

Esther, and selections from *Joshua*, *The Redemption*, *Jephtha*, *Samson*, *Judas Maccabæus*, and the *Dettingen Te Deum* were to be given.

On the first evening, selections from Mozart's *La Clemenza di Tito* by Madame Macaroni, and the overture to *Anacreon*, were gone through.

On the second morning (1st November), the *Messiah* was given; on the second evening, amongst other things, the overture to *Zauberflöte*.

On the third morning, 'Total Eclipse' (Handel) was an item; on the third evening, a Grand Symphony (Mozart) and a March by Haydn were part of the performance.

On the fourth morning, the overture to *Samson*, the overture to *Saul*, Beethoven's *Mount of Olives*, and a piece of Pergolesi's were given.

The detailed history of all the Musical Societies of Edinburgh since 1815 would fall far beyond the scope of this little work; but as some may be interested to see how they connect with the famous ancestor of them all, whose life-work we have been studying, we may epitomise in the following manner[1] what may be called the modern period:—

In 1819, 'The Edinburgh Professional Society of Musicians' was established; and in 1831, 'The Phil-

[1] The substance of two articles in the *Scotsman* of December 28 and 29, 1893.

harmonic Society of Leith' was inaugurated, being composed of both vocalists and instrumentalists under the leadership of R. B. Stewart.

Between 1830 and 1835, in addition to the two above mentioned, there were 'The Choral Society' and 'The Edinburgh St. Cecilia Amateur Orchestral Society.' These two occasionally united their forces when a more than usually ambitious concert was to be attempted.

This St. Cecilia Orchestral Society contained no professional member except the conductor. At first it usually met in the Hopetoun Rooms in Queen Street (now part of the Edinburgh Ladies' College), but later the Clyde Street Hall was the scene of its gatherings. Practisings were held once a week—usually on Wednesdays, and not earlier than 8 P.M. Each evening's work overtook at least two symphonies of Haydn, Mozart, or Beethoven, and two overtures of Mozart, Rossini, or Auber.

Two names, very interesting to us now, occur in the list of members—Sir Thomas Dick Lauder's and Mr. (now Sir) Douglas Maclagan's. Lord Barriedale was a member. This Society gave two concerts in the season 1845-46 for the benefit of the Royal Infirmary, by the former of which they handed over £152, 12s. 2d., and by the latter £71, 5s. 10d. to the funds of that noble institution.

Though the Assembly Rooms in George Street were

built between 1783 and 1787, the Music Hall behind was not opened until 1843.

And now our sketch is finished, with the full sense that it is but an unfinished sketch. We have told a tale of other days—days differing in many respects from our own; but the same music that rang out its sweetness when St. Cecilia's was the *new* concert-hall is still ours most fully to enjoy—such is the ever-freshness of true art.

A task taken up only from time to time, during holidays and on occasions separated by long intervals of very different occupation, must of necessity seem somewhat of a patchwork. Of this and many other shortcomings the author is painfully conscious. More might have been discovered by one with greater leisure, much might have been better told; but not a line could have been written by any one who loves more fervently Edinburgh—queen of cities—and her romantic story. The holiday task has been a labour of love, and the labourer will have been rewarded could he know that he has given him who is a stranger to the city some fresh facts of interest, or him who has the privilege of having been born within her gates or within sight of her towers, one new link in the chain of old associations that binds her sons throughout the world yet nearer to herself.

APPENDIX I

EXTRACTS FROM THE SEDERUNT-BOOK OF THE DEAN OF GUILD COURT, EDINBURGH.

EDINBURGH, *the twenty-eighth day of November, seventeen hundred and fifty-nine years.*

Sederunt.

JOHN CARMICHAELL, D.G.	PATRICK JAMESON.
JAMES ROBERTSON.	HUGH INGLIS.
	CHARLES HOUISON.

Petition for the Edinburgh Musical Society for warrant to build a Concert Hall on an area purchased by them lying near the foot of Niddery's Wynd. The Deacon and Box-master of Mary's Chappel, and James Thomson and Mr. Andrew being all present, Crave to see and answer, which the Court allow and assign Monday next for that effect.

(BORROWING RECEIPT.)

EDINBURGH, 20*th November* 1759.

Borrowed up the Petition for the Musical Society for warrant to build in Niddery's Wynd, with plan relative to.

JAMES WILSON.

> EDINBURGH, *the fifth day of December, seventeen hundred and fifty-nine years.*

Sederunt.

JOHN CARMICHAELL, D.G., ETC.

In the Petition for the Musical Society. The Court assign this day fourteen days peremptorie to the haill neighbouring heretors to produce any servitude they have on the ground craved to be built upon, or any part thereof.

JOHN CARMICHAELL, D.G.

> EDINBURGH, *the nineteenth day of December, one thousand seven hundred and fifty-nine.*

Sederunt.

JOHN CARMICHAELL, D.G., ETC.

In the Petition for the Musical Society for warrant to build. The Court, in respect there is no servitude produced by the contiguous heretors on the area before mentioned: They therefore circumduce the term against them for not producing, and appoint a visit.

> EDINBURGH, *the ninth day of January, seventeen hundred and sixty years.*

Sederunt.

JOHN CARMICHAELL, D.G.	PATRICK JAMESON.
JAMES ROBERTSON.	HUGH INGLIS.
GEORGE PITCAIRN.	CHARLES HOUISON.

In the Petition for the Musical Society for warrant to build a Concert Hall. The Court having considered the petition and plan of the Society's ground produced, and having visited the said ground and heard the answers for the Incorporation of Mary's Chappel, they grant the warrant to the Musical Society to build their Concert Hall on the area mentioned in the petition, they preserving the syver or watergang running from the property of the said Incorporation, so as to have a free course down to the Cowgate, and making no entry or communication from their said property into that of the Incorporations as mentioned in the answers, and likewise observing the Acts made anent building within the city of Edinburgh.

JOHN CARMICHAELL, D.G.

To the Honourable the Lord Dean of Guild
and his Council.

The Petition of the Musical Society at Edinburgh

Sheweth that your petitioners propose to put up an iron rail[1] in front of their property before their hall in Niddry Wynd : your petitioners therefore pray the Court will give authority for doing the same.

WILLIAM DOUGLAS, Treasurer.

EDINBURGH, 6th September 1764.

The Court having considered the petition, appoint the contiguous heretors to be summoned to next court day, and in the meantime appoint a visit.

PATRICK LINDESAY, D.G.
(The Honourable Patrick Lindesay.)

---

[1] The pillars shown in plan of the ground-floor, p. 28, had possibly to do with this iron rail. The railing may have run from the pillars to the houses north and south of the entrance.

APPENDIX II

Copy of Petition (*with Plan attached*) lodged in the Dean of Guild Court, Edinburgh.

5th March 1812.

Unto the Honourable the Lord Dean of Guild of Edinburgh and his Council, the Petition of William Inglis, Esquire, Writer to the Signet, and Alexander Lawrie, Bookseller and Stationer in Edinburgh,

Humbly sheweth,—

That the Petitioners are Disponees in trust for behoof of the Grand Lodge of Free Masons of Scotland of that large building at the foot of Niddry's Street, Edinburgh, formerly called St. Cecilia's Hall, now Free Masons' Hall, and the piece of vacant ground lying on the south of said hall the length of Cowgate Street.

That the Petitioners propose building on said piece of vacant ground conform to a plan and elevation herewith produced, but before doing so they make the present application for the sanction of your Lordship and Council.

May it therefore please your Lordships and Council to appoint the Conterminous Heritors to be summoned, and thereafter to grant warrant to the Petitioners to build conform to the plan herewith produced; and in the event of any of the conterminous heritors making unnecessary opposition, to find such of them liable in expense.

According to Justice,

(*Signed*) GEORGE CARPHIN.

2nd April 1812.

Having visited and considered the titles produced in respect of no objections from any of the conterminous heritors, grant warrant to the Petitioners to build in terms of the prayer of the petition and plan produced, which is relative hereto, the building not to extend further south than that on the west side of Niddry Street; and decerns.

(*Signed*) KINCAID MACKENZIE, D.G.

APPENDIX III

TRANSCRIPT of a rare eighteen-page pamphlet in the possession of Mr. Robert A. Marr, consisting of a list of the members of the Musical Society at Edinburgh as on May 1, 1775.

A

LIST

OF THE

MEMBERS

OF THE

MUSICAL SOCIETY

AT

EDINBURGH.

MAY I.   M,DCC,LXXV.

Appendices

A

LIST

OF

GOVERNORS

AND

DIRECTORS.

THE RIGHT HONOURABLE
THE EARL OF HADINTON. } *Governor.*

THE RIGHT HONOURABLE
THE EARL OF KELLY. } *Deputy-Governor.*

MR. JOHN WELSH, Clerk to the Signet, *Treasurer.*

SIR WILLIAM FORBES, Baronet,
ALEXANDER WIGHT, Esq., Advocate,
ROBERT SINCLAIR, Esq., Advocate,
MR. SAMUEL MITCHELSON, } Clerks to the
MR. WILLIAM TYTLER, } Signet,
ARCHIBALD GRANT, Esq.,
    One Vacant. } *Directors.*

LIST, &c.

A

His Grace the Duke of Argyle.
Right Hon. the Earl of Aberdeen.
    Sir John Anstruther, Bart.
    Alexander Abercrombie, Esq., Advocate.
    Mr. William Anderson, Writer.

B

His Grace the Duke of Buccleugh.
Right Hon. the Earl of Breadalbine.
Right Hon. the Earl of Balcarras.
Hon. Robert Bruce, Esq., Lord Kennet.
    Lord Binning.
    Dr. Black.
    William Berry, Esq.
    George Buchan-Hepburn, Esq., Advocate.
    Charles Brown, Esq., Advocate.
    Claud Boswell, Esq., Advocate.
    George Brown of Illieston, Esq.
    George Buchan of Kelly, Esq.
    John Balfour of Balbirnie, Esq.
    Mr. James Balmain, Sollicitor of Excise.
    Mr. Charles Brown, Clerk to the Signet.
    Mr. John Bell, Clerk to the Signet.

C

Right Hon. the Earl of Cassilis.
Hon. Francis Charteris, Esq.
    Sir James Clerk of Pennycuik, Bart.
    Daniel Campbell of Shawfield, Esq.
    Thomas Craig of Riccarton, Esq.
    Mr. Alexander Cunyngham, Clerk to the Signet.
    Robert Chalmers, Esq.
    Ilay Campbell, Esq., Advocate.
    Andrew Crosbie, Esq., Advocate.
    Mr. David Craigie, Clerk to the Signet.
    George Clerk-Maxwell, Commissioner of the Customs.
    Robert Cullen, Esq., Advocate.
    James Colquhoun, Esq., Advocate.

George Clerk, Esq., Advocate.
Colonel Campbell of Finab.
James Cheap of Sauchie, Esq.

D

Right Hon. the Earl of Dumfries.
Right Hon. the Earl of Dalhousie.
Right Hon. the Earl of Dunmore.
Right Hon. Robert Dundas, Esq., Lord President of the Court of Session.
Hon. Sir David Dalrymple, Lord Hailes.
John Dalrymple, Esq., Merchant.
Mr. John Davidson, Clerk to the Signet.
James Dundas of Dundas, Esq., Sollicitor.
Henry Dundas, Esq., Sollicitor.
Thomas Dundas of Castlecary, Esq.

E

Right Hon. the Lord Elibank.
Hon. James Erskine, Lord Alva.
Alexander Elphingston, Esq., Advocate.
Mr. Thomas Elder, Merchant.

F

Right Hon. the Earl of Fife.
Sir William Forbes, Bart.
James Ferguson, younger of Pitfour, Esq.
William Fullerton, Esq., of Carstairs.
William Fullerton, Esq., of Rosemont.
George Ferguson, Esq., Advocate.
Alexander Ferguson, Esq., Advocate.
Mr. George Fairholm, Merchant.
William Fullerton of Fullerton, Esq.

G

His Grace the Duke of Gordon.
Hon. Mr. Baron Grant.
Hon. Alexander Gordon, Esq., Advocate.
    Sir Alexander Gilmour, Bart.
    Captain Archibald Grant of Monimusk.
    Cosmo Gordon, Esq., Advocate.
    Thomas Graham of Balgowan, Esq.
    Mr. William Grant.
    Mr. James Geddes.
    Mr. Gordon Kinloch.
    Mr. John Gardner.

H

Right Hon. the Earl of Hadinton.
Right Hon. the Earl of Hyndford.
Right Hon. Lord Hope.
Hon. Henry Hume, Esq., Lord Kaimes.
Hon. Charles Hope-Vere, Esq.
    General Horn.
    John Hamilton of Bargeny, Esq.
    Patrick Hume, Esq., of Wedderburne.
    William Hall of Whitehall, Esq.
    Dr. Francis Home.
    Mr. Walter Hamilton, Merchant.
    Robert Hepburn of Clerkington, Esq.
    Matthew Henderson, Esq.
    Mr. James Hunter, Merchant.
    Thomas Hogg, Esq., Advocate.
    Mr. George Home, Clerk to the Signet.
    George Home of Kaimes, Esq.
    James Hamilton of Bangour, Esq.
    Robert Hunter, Esq.
    Dr. James Hay.

Appendices

I

Sir John Inglis, Baronet.
Mr. Patrick Inglis, Merchant.
Mr. Gilbert Innes.
Alexander Johnston of Straiton.

K

Right Hon. the Earl of Kelly.
Lord Kilmaurs.
    David Kennedy, Esq., Advocate.
    David Kinloch of Gilmerton, Esq.
    Mr. William Kirkpatrick, Clerk of Session.
    Mr. Patrick Ker, Clerk to the Signet.
    Mr. James Ker.
    Mr. Alexander Keith, Clerk to the Signet.
    Alexander Kincaid, jun., Esq.

L

Right Hon. the Earl of Leven.
    General Lockhart.
    Captain Lockhart of Castlehill.
    Dr. James Lind.
    Mr. Patrick Lindesay, Merchant.

M

Honourable Mr. Baron Maule.
Honourable Mr. Baron Mure.
Right Hon. Thomas Miller, Lord Justice-Clerk.
Right Hon. James Montgomery, Lord Advocate.
    Mr. Samuel Mitchelson, Clerk to the Signet.
    Mr. Alexander Maxwell, Merchant.
    William Macdowall of Castlesemple, Esq.
    Mr. George Mure, Clerk of Justiciary.

Patrick Murray, Esq., Advocate.
Mr. John Macgowan, Writer.
David Stewart-Moncrieffe, Esq.
Mr. John Mackenzie, Clerk to the Signet.
Mr. Patrick Miller, Merchant.
Robert Macqueen, Esq., Advocate.
Alexander Murray, Esq., Advocate.
Archibald Menzies of Culdares, Esq.
John Mackenzie, Esq., of Dolphinton.
Henry Mackenzie, Esq.
Sir William Maxwell, Bart.
Mr. Duncan M'Millan.
William Murray of Touchaddam, Esq.
Mr. Allan M'Connochie, Advocate.
Mr. M'Leod of M'Leod.

N

William Nisbet of Dirleton, Esq.
William Nairne, Esq., Advocate.
William Nisbet, junior, of Dirleton, Esq.

O

Right Hon. Robert Orde, Esq., Lord Chief Baron of Exchequer.
Archibald Ogilvie of Inchmartin, Esq.
Robert Oliphant, Esq., of Rossie.
General Oughton.
Mr. George Ogilvie, Advocate.

P

Mr. John Pringle, Clerk to the Signet.
Mr. James Pringle, Clerk of Session.
John Pringle, Esq., Advocate.

Appendices

Q

R

His Grace the Duke of Roxburgh.
Right Hon. the Earl of Roseberry.
    David Ross, Esq., Advocate.
    David Rae, Esq., Advocate.
    Mr. John Russel, Clerk to the Signet.
    Mr. Alex. Robertson, Clerk to the Signet.
    Roger Robertson, Esq.
    Mr. James Rae, Surgeon.
    Dr. Ramsay.
    John Cuming-Ramsay, Esq., Advocate.
    Mr. David Russell, Accomptant.
    Mr. John Russell, junior.
    John Rutherford, Esq.
    Mr. Munro Ross, Advocate.

S

Right Hon. the Earl of Selkirk.
    Sir George Suttie of Balgone, Bart.
    Walter Scott of Harden, Esq.
    Hugh Seton of Touch, Esq.
    John Swinton, Esq., Advocate.
    Robert Sinclair, Esq., Advocate.
    David Smith, Esq., of Methuen.
    Andrew Stewart, Esq.
    Charles Sharp, Esq., of Hoddam.
    Alexander Scrymgeour, Esq., Advocate.
    Mr. Francis Strachan, Clerk to the Signet.
    Francis Scott, Esq.

Colonel Skene.
Mr. James Stewart, Clerk to the Signet.
Mr. David Stewart, Clerk to the Signet.
Mr. James Stirling, Merchant.
Mr. James Spence, Writer.
Mr. Schaw Stewart.

T

Mr. William Tytler, Clerk to the Signet.
Mr. Alexander Tait, Clerk of Session.
Alexander Telfer of Symington, Esq.
Alexander Tytler, Esq., Advocate.
John Trotter, younger of Mortonhall.

U

Alexander Udny of Udny, Esq.

V

W

Hon. James Wemyss of Wemyss, Esq.
John Wauchope of Edmonstone, Esq.
Sir John Whiteford, Baronet.
The Rev. Dr. George Wishart.
William Wallace, Esq., Advocate.
Alexander Wight, Esq., Advocate.
Thomas Wharton, Esq., Commissioner of Excise.
George Wallace, Esq., Advocate.
Mr. John Welsh, Clerk to the Signet.
Robert Whytt, Esq., Advocate.
Sir Thomas Wallace, Baronet.

Appendices

Mr. John Wordie.
Mr. Wellwood of Garvock.
Mr. Wait.

X

Y

Dr. Thomas Young.

Z

INDEX

ABEL, KARL F., 180.
Amateurs, musical, in 1695, 251.
Aragoni (Arrigoni), 77, 221.
Arne, Thomas Augustine, Mus. Doc., 111, 115.
Arnot's account of St. Cecilia Concerts, 203.
Artaxerxes performed in Edinburgh in 1769, 113.

BACH, J. S., 160.
Barnard, Mr., 79.
Barsanti, F., 170.
Bassani, G. B., 166.
Bell, Dr. Benjamin, 11.
Beethoven, 161.
Blacklock, Dr., 224.
'Boar Club' founded, 74.
Boccherini, 60.
Bocchi, L., 263.
Bremner, R., 122.
Brent, Miss, 113.
Burnet, Elizabeth, 226.
Burney, Dr., 135.
Burns, Miss (*alias* Matthews), 237.
Burns, Robert, arrival in Edinburgh, 224.

CAMPBELL, JOHN, AND ALEXANDER, 114.
Chalmers, Margaret ('Peggy'), 232.

'Clarinda,' 69, 241.
Clarke, S., 99.
Cockburn, Lord, on St. Cecilia's Concert, 213.
Concert on St. Cecilia's Day 1695, 250.
Concerts in Canongate and Cowgate, 277.
Concerts, various kinds of, in Old Edinburgh, 218.
Corelli, A., 165.
Corri, Domenico, 131.
—— Natali, 107, 141, 143.
Corri's Rooms, 142, 281.
Craig, Adam, 253.
Cramer, Wilhelm, 95.
—— J. B., 96, 181.
Cross Keys Tavern, 204, 259.

DOMENICHINO, 41.
Drummore, Lord, 154, 206, 209.
Duc de Berri at a St. Cecilia Concert, 247.

FERGUSSON, ROBERT, 11.
Ferrier, Miss, 240.
Festival, Edinburgh Musical, in 1815, 281.
Fortune's Tavern, 216.
French princes exiles at Holyrood, 67.

GEMINIANI, F., 169.
Gibson, Cornforth, 150, 221.
Giornovicki, G. M., 80, 161.
Glencairn, Earl of, 231.
Gluck, 161.
Gordon, Duchess of, 229.
Gordon, Mr., gives concerts, 255.
Grange, Lord, 7.
—— 'Lady,' 7.
Guarnerius, a violin by, 95.
Guglielmi, P., 185.

HAMILTON, CHARLOTTE, 232.
Handel, G. F., 160, 204, 205, 206.
Haydn, 160.
Hesse, Prince of, at a St. Cecilia Concert, 209.
Holyrood, Schetky at concerts at, 67.
Hopetoun, Earl of, 114, 154.

INDEX as at 1782 of Musical Society, 161.

JAMES VII. in Edinburgh, 248.

KELLY, SIXTH EARL OF, 157.
Kincaid on St. Cecilia's Concert, 211.

LADIES at the St. Cecilia Concerts, 243.
Lampe, Johann Friedrich, 265.
—— Mrs., 266.
Lampe's tomb in Canongate Churchyard, 267.

M'DONALD, PENELOPE, 242.

M'Gibbon, William, and Matthew, 254.
Macleod, Isabella, 242.
Maitland on origin of Musical Society of Edinburgh, 194.
Marchetti, Mrs., 80.
Members of Musical Society at 1775, 199.
Metastasio, 173.
Mozart, 111, 161.
Murray, Euphemia, 233.
Mylne, Robert, architect of St. Cecilia's, 42.
Mylne, family of, Royal Master-Masons, 46.

NIDDRY, antiquity of name, 4.

OLIPHANT, CAROLINE, 239.
Olivieri, 119.
Orchestra of St. Cecilia's in 1774, 106.
Organ of St. Cecilia's Hall, 222.
Oswald, J., 192.
—— Mrs. R. A., 236.
O'Keefe on Tenducci, 115.

PAGANINI, 80.
Paisiello, G., 186.
Parma, opera-house at, 2.
Pasquale, Signor and Signora, 268.
Passerini, Signor and Signora, 272.
Pinto, T., 77.
Pitcairne, Dr. Archibald, 260.
Pleyel, I. J., 182.
Poole, Miss (Mrs. Dickons), 148.
Puppo, Giuseppe, 57.

Index

RAMSAY, ALLAN, on Musical Club, 191.
Reinagle, Joseph, 76.
—— Joseph (son), 76.
Riddell, Maria, 234.

ST. CECILIA THE MARTYR, 40.
St. Cecilia, Feast of, 41.
St. Cecilia Concerts ended, 278.
St. Cecilia's Hall, 13.
St. John's Chapel, Canongate, 73.
St. Mary's Chapel, 9.
Sarti, G., 189.
'Saving the ladies,' 210.
Schetky, J. G. C., 60.
—— John C. (son), 63.
Scott, Sir Walter, 143, 144, 244.
—— Walter, senior, 245.
Siddons, Mrs., 99.
Smollett on St. Mary's Chapel Concert, 199.
Stabilini, G. or H., 84, 107.
Stamitz, J., 178.
—— C., 179.

Steil (Steel), Pate, 204, 259.
Stewart, Anne, 241.
Subscription, annual, to Musical Society, 276.

TENDUCCI, G. F., 108, 202, 222.
—— Signora, 113, 117.
Thomson, Daniel, and William, 252.
Thomson, George, 51.
—— —— on St. Cecilia Concerts, 214.
Thomson, James, 177.
Topham on St. Cecilia Concerts, 201.

URBANI, PIETRO, 123.

VANHALL, J. B., 181.
Vogel's concert, one of the last, in 1798, 246.

WILSON, SIR DANIEL, on St. Cecilia's Hall, 218.

Printed by T. and A. CONSTABLE, Printers to Her Majesty
at the Edinburgh University Press

www.ingramcontent.com/pod-product-compliance
Lightning Source LLC
Chambersburg PA
CBHW022022240426
43667CB00042B/1060